THE BOTANICAL GARDENS

AT THE HUNTINGTON

Principal Photographer
DON NORMARK

Supervising Editor
PEGGY PARK BERNAL

HUNTINGTON LIBRARY
SAN MARINO, CALIFORNIA

Third edition
The text of the first edition, by Walter Houk with captions by Rosemary Verey, has been amended and amplified by the Huntington botanical staff for this new edition.

Director and Curators of the Botanical Division

James P. Folsom, Marge and Sherm Telleen Director of the Botanical Gardens
Dylan Hannon, Curator, Conservatory and Tropical Collections
T. June Li, Curator, Liu Fang Yuan
Gary Lyons, Curator, Desert Garden
David MacLaren, Curator, Asian Gardens
Clair Martin III, Ruth B. and E. L. Shannon Curator, Rose and Perennial Gardens
Kathy Musial, Curator, Living Collections, and Collections Manager
Shadi Shihab, Curator, Floristic Gardens
John Trager, Curator, Desert Collections

Printed in China
ISBN 978-0-87328-238-3

Library of Congress Cataloging in Publication Data
The Botanical Gardens at the Huntington / by Huntington Botanical Staff ; principal photographer, Don Normark ; supervising editor, Peggy Park Bernal.—2nd ed., rev. and expanded
    p.   cm.
  Includes index.
  Rev. ed. of The Botanical Gardens at the Huntington / by Walter Houk … [et al.]. c1996
  ISBN 0-87328-215-9 (pbk. : alk. paper)
  1. Huntington Botanical Gardens. 2. Huntington Botanical Gardens–Pictorial works.
I. Normark, Don, 1928– II. Bernal, Peggy Park, 1939– III. Houk, Walter, Botanical Gardens at the Huntington. IV. Huntington Botanical Gardens.
    QK73.U62H866 2006
    580. 73'79493—dc22   2005029819
            CIP

FRONT COVER: Scenic view looking south from Liu Fang Yuan toward the Pavilion for Washing Away Thoughts.

BACK COVER: Palms and cycads line a walkway from the waterfall to the Huntington Gallery.

FRONTISPIECE: Landscaping at the public entrances—this is one of two—is a preview of the plants visitors will see in the main gardens beyond.

PAGES 2–3: The Library setting is tranquil and elegant, with a broad expanse of luxuriant lawn in front and the majestic San Gabriel Mountains in back.

TITLE PAGE: The North Vista, lined with statues, stately palms, and mounds of azaleas, is a favorite photographic subject for visitors.

Historic photos are from the Huntington's photograph collections.

All other photographs copyright © Don Normark, except as follows:

page 21, bottom: Advanced Digital Maps Incorporated
page 37: Lisa Blackburn
pages 54-55: Bonnie Muench
page 56, top and bottom left: Joe Clements
page 58, right: Bonnie Muench
page 62: Joe Clements
page 63, top: Joe Clements
page 64 bottom left and right: Joe Clements
page 67, top: Kit Amorn
page 67, bottom: John N. Trager
page 68: John N. Trager
page 69: John N. Trager
page 92, bottom right: Judy Danner
page 94, left: Ann Richardson
page 95: Grady Perigan
page 115: Warren Hill
page 117: John Sullivan
page 130: John N. Trager
page 131, top left, bottom: John N. Trager
page 146, top and bottom right: Noramelia Martinez
page 147: Noramelia Martinez
page 151, bottom: Bonnie Muench
page 153: John Sullivan
page 154, top, bottom left and right: Clair Martin III
page 157, top, left and right, bottom, left: Lisa Blackburn
pages 158–65: John Sullivan
page 188: Robert Schlosser
page 191: Gerald R. Fredrick
page 196, column 1, center right: Ann Richardson
page 196, column 2, bottom left: Joe Clements
page 197, column 1, top: James P. Folsom
page 197, column 1, center left and right; column 2, top left and right: John N. Trager

Huntington Library Press
1151 Oxford Road
San Marino, CA 91108
www.huntington.org

Susan Green, Director
Jean Patterson, Managing Editor

Contents

· A MESSAGE FROM THE PRESIDENT ·

THE DYNAMIC NATURE of the Huntington is most visible in its gardens as they change from season to season. From the vivid blues and greens of the desert puyas in the spring to the still, quiet beauty of the gingko trees in autumn, the Huntington Botanical Gardens provide a feast for the senses. The gardens occupy 120 acres of the Huntington estate, one of the last remaining properties of this size and scale in Los Angeles County. The plants growing here—many of them rare or endangered—are organized into individual gardens that represent themed landscapes and cultural traditions.

The gardens represent a serious botanical enterprise, yes, with curators, horticulturists, and botanists working hand in glove with gardeners and volunteers to maintain, propagate, protect, study, and celebrate the collections. But along with this, they offer an extraordinary aesthetic experience, providing a place of refuge from the intensely urban landscape of Los Angeles—a retreat, a place for reflection.

And yet, at the same time, the Huntington bustles with excitement and forward motion. With the expansion of its research and educational programming has come some important new developments: the 16,000-square-foot Rose Hills Conservatory for Botanical Science and the Helen and Peter Bing Children's Garden help children make a direct connection between the grandeur of the gardens and the science behind them. Today at the Huntington, children explore interactive kinetic sculptures and puzzle through inquiry-based plant exhibits, adults learn about plant biodiversity and other subjects in workshops, and science teachers study new ways to excite and engage their students in the endless wonders of botany.

We hope this book inspires you to learn more about plants, botanical science, and the Huntington's gardens. For information on current activities, visit our Web site at www.huntington.org.

STEVEN KOBLIK
President

This landmark glass-and-steel conservatory housing interactive exhibits is now the Huntington's cornerstone for science education.

· FOREWORD ·

Henry Edwards Huntington purchased James De Barth Shorb's San Marino Ranch in 1903, flush with enthusiasm for the accommodating climate and the economic future of Southern California. Although he did not arrive with a plan for developing the property, he knew from previous visits to the ranch that this land near Pasadena would support cultivation of oranges and peaches, palms and roses. Huntington brought to the project a passion for development that united his expanding avocations—building great literary, research, art, and plant collections, examining the bountiful horticultural and agricultural potential of the local climate, and creating the structure and resources for his dynamic legacy—the Huntington Library, Art Collections, and Botanical Gardens.

The Huntington Botanical Gardens respond to his vision still today. Even as we face changing times with newly apparent environmental, social, and economic concerns, the values of plants and gardens as well as the importance of botanical, horticultural, and agricultural investigation remain fundamental and undiminished. Mr. Huntington appreciated the basic need to press ahead with the study and explanation of the nature and importance of plants. As part of an educational museum and research institution, the gardens strive to serve the public welfare through continuing dedication to that mission.

James Folsom
Marge and Sherm Telleen Director of the Botanical Gardens

This detailed illustration of the tropical orchid *Sobralia macrantha* appeared in James Bateman's *Orchidaceae of Mexico and Guatamala* (1842), one of many rare volumes in the Huntington's botanical library.

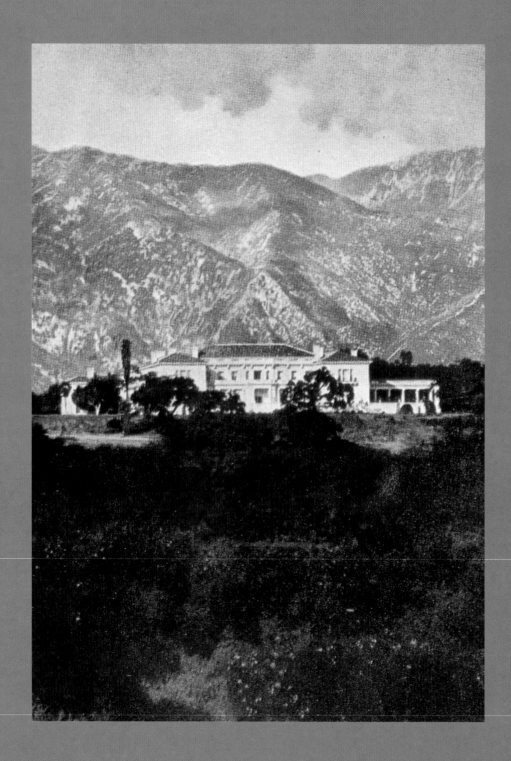

· HISTORIC OVERVIEW ·
NATURE'S BEAUTY ENHANCED BY MAN'S DESIGN

SOME VISITORS see the Huntington estate as one of the world's most beautiful gardens. Some see it as a living museum of the rare and wonderful in the world of plants, a laboratory for the pursuit of botanical and horticultural knowledge. Some see it as a princely repository of books and paintings amid decorous lawns and groves. All the above views are valid. The Huntington's remarkable synergy of literature, art, and nature creates a whole that is far greater than the sum of its parts. This book will focus on the garden part, but first let us take a look at that magical whole.

Founded in 1919 by Henry Edwards Huntington, the Huntington Library, Art Collections, and Botanical Gardens is an educational and cultural center serving both scholars and the general public. Opened to the public in 1928, the year after its owner died, this renowned legacy is an assemblage of collections unique in the world, inviting comparison with any great house in Europe or America.

The Huntington Library is one of the largest and most complete research libraries in America in the fields of British and American history, literature, and science. It contains more than 800,000 books and close to six million manuscripts, including such

LEFT: This view of the Huntington mansion was the frontispiece for the 1915 book *Stately Homes of California* by Porter Garnett. He described the house as "the most 'palatial' residence in California" and the gardens "in outdoor plants, among the richest in the world."

Heart-shaped sprinkler head

LEFT: Henry Edwards Huntington amassed a fortune as a railroad and real estate developer, then spent some of it assembling major collections of rare books, manuscripts, paintings, and plants.

MIDDLE: Arabella Duval Huntington married Henry Huntington in 1913; she was previously married to his uncle Collis, who died in 1900. She and Henry were close in age and had many interests in common.

RIGHT: Henry E. Huntington and his uncle Collis P. Huntington (right), photographed on a San Francisco street in the 1890s.

treasures as the Ellesmere manuscript of Chaucer's *Canterbury Tales* (c. 1400), a Gutenberg Bible (c. 1455), and the manuscript of Benjamin Franklin's *Autobiography,* one of the most important documents in American history. The Munger Research Center, opened in 2004, houses state-of-the-art laboratories for conservation, photography, and digital imaging as well as research offices and storage for rare books and manuscripts.

The art collections are housed in four galleries. A fifth space, the MaryLou and George Boone Gallery, presents changing exhibitions. The Huntington Gallery, originally the estate residence, contains one of America's most distinguished collections of British paintings and sculpture of the eighteenth and early nineteenth centuries, as well as outstanding eighteenth-century French decorative art. Its famed paintings include Thomas Gainsborough's *The Blue Boy,* Sir Thomas Lawrence's *Pinkie*, and Sir Joshua Reynolds's *Sarah Siddons as the Tragic Muse*. The Virginia Steele Scott Gallery of American Art exhibits American paintings from the eighteenth to the twentieth centuries, as well as work by noted Pasadena architects Charles and Henry Greene and artisans of the early-twentieth-century Arts and Crafts movement. The nearby Lois and Robert F. Erburu Gallery, opened in 2005, provides additional exhibition space for the expanding collection of American art. A gallery in the Library displays

LEFT: Known as the Big Red Cars, the trolleys of Pacific Electric handled thousands of commuters every day and offered such special sightseeing trips as the one advertised in this brochure for a visit to the "Orange Kingdom."

RIGHT: Streetcars, automobiles, and horse-drawn buggies share Colorado Boulevard in Pasadena in 1910.

the Arabella Huntington Memorial Collection of Renaissance paintings and eighteenth-century French sculpture and decorative arts.

Surrounding the buildings are 120 acres of gardens with sweeping lawns and vistas, graced by pavilions, pergolas, arbors, fountains, ponds, statuary, decorative tempiettos ("little temples"), and such other structures as the Huntington mausoleum in the tempietto form. The grounds are luxuriant with 15,000 different kinds of plants from the world over, displayed as botanical and landscape subjects in separate gardens.

Such diverse collections reflect the extraordinary range of interests of Henry Huntington, a railroad and real estate developer who had enormous impact on Southern California in the early twentieth century. His Pacific Electric Railway, incorporated in 1901, grew into a vast street-rail and interurban rapid transit system, defining patterns of settlement that would structure the future Los Angeles metropolis and indeed predict its freeway network. As his rail lines expanded, he also bought, developed, and sold property along their rights of way to amass the largest landholdings in Southern California and greatly enlarge an inherited fortune.

He achieved most of that in little more than the decade before he retired from

This ground plan of San Marino Ranch in 1904 shows areas devoted to oranges, peaches, apricots, pepper trees, and a plot described as "mixed orchard." Existing structures, including a residence, barns, bunkhouse, and tanks, are also indicated.

business in 1910. Meanwhile, starting in 1903 he devoted more than two decades to developing the country place we know today simply as "The Huntington."

The complex occupies an astonishing site on an eminence above the San Gabriel Valley east of Los Angeles. Like a stage backdrop, the awesomely steep San Gabriel Mountains, snow-capped in winter, tower to the north. To the south the property commands a sweeping view over the broad valley and on the clearest days to the sea beyond the Los Angeles plain.

Huntington's gardens grew out of Southern California's golden age of horticulture from the late nineteenth century well into the twentieth. During that time wave after wave of newcomers, captivated by the mild Mediterranean climate, transformed this favored land into a tour de force of landscaping with plant material from the world over. In developing his estate Huntington wanted his collections to yield information, ever enlarging the vocabulary of landscape art while increasing scientific knowledge.

By the turn of the century Southern California was full of plant enthusiasts from the East and Europe, all happily trying out what would thrive here. The U.S. Department of Agriculture joined in the worldwide search, bringing back test material for its own experiment stations and for distribution to individuals, nurseries, park

The three-story Victorian mansion of James De Barth Shorb was a mecca for prominent visitors, including Henry Huntington, who was a guest there in 1892. Huntington built his own mansion on the same site eighteen years later.

departments, arboreta, and gardens. In time it would give more than five thousand plants to the Huntington.

BORN IN 1850 in Oneonta, New York, Henry Edwards Huntington left home at age twenty to work for a New York hardware supplier. Before long his uncle, railroad baron Collis P. Huntington, recruited him to manage a West Virginia railroad-tie sawmill. Ten years later Collis appointed him construction superintendent of the Chesapeake, Ohio and South Western Railroad in Kentucky and in a few years made him manager of the Kentucky Central. By 1890 the railroad world recognized two Huntingtons, calling the younger "H. E." to distinguish him from the more famous "C. P."

In the spring of 1892 Henry made his first trip to California. He was headed for the San Francisco headquarters of the Southern Pacific Company, the SP, the powerful holding company for the Southern Pacific and Central Pacific railroads. Henry would be special assistant to the SP president, Collis Huntington. Traveling in C. P.'s private railroad car, the two Huntingtons took the Southern Pacific Railroad, southernmost of the transcontinental lines, giving H. E. his first look at that operation. A stopover in Los Angeles gave him his first glimpse of Southern California.

Landowner James De Barth Shorb extended his hospitality during the

Henry Huntington rests beside an oak saved by tree surgery, its cavities filled with steel-reinforced concrete. William Hertrich wrote, "There was no subject Mr. Huntington loved to discuss ... more than the trees he had been able to save."

Huntingtons' brief stay in 1892. History mostly remembers Shorb as the son-in-law of Benjamin Davis Wilson, a Yankee pioneer who became a major landholder, businessman, and first mayor of Los Angeles. Among Wilson's properties was one called Lake Vineyard, seven miles northeast of Los Angeles and fertile with grapes, oranges, olives, figs, and half a dozen other orchard crops. He had given Shorb part of it, called Mount Vineyard, and under Shorb's stewardship both became well known. Shorb renamed his ranch "San Marino" after his boyhood home in Maryland.

AFTER THAT VISIT with the Shorbs in 1892, Henry Huntington went on to San Francisco and his position as a high official at Southern Pacific. With his wife and four children, he led an active and socially prominent life for several years. When C. P. died in 1900, H. E. inherited a fortune, but his hope of succeeding his uncle as company president was thwarted when he was outvoted by stockholders. He decided to withdraw from management.

Thus at the turn of the century Huntington turned his attention to Southern California, which he accurately saw as a land of promise. Here his major business

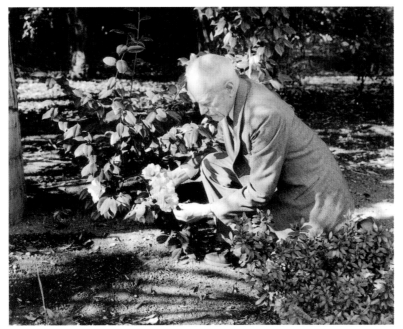

William Hertrich, superintendent of the Huntington Botanical Gardens from 1905 to 1948, examining the blossoms of a camellia. Hertrich authored several books and articles on plants, including a three-volume work on camellias in the Huntington gardens. He was a prominent authority and received numerous awards from national and international organizations for his horticultural contributions.

accomplishment would be a rail empire he had begun in 1898 with the acquisition of the Los Angeles Railway, the LARY. He soon acquired other lines in and around Los Angeles, eventually integrating a hundred traction companies into the Pacific Electric, the PE, the largest interurban network in the world. In its heyday, PE's literature boasted of 2,700 scheduled trolleys and trains a day and its standard-gauge, horn-blowing Big Red Cars rumbled over more than a thousand miles of track.

Huntington built power generating and other utilities for his electric railways and for the real estate that he coordinated with his rail systems. He left his name all over the map, on the towns of Huntington Beach and Huntington Park, on such districts as Huntington Palisades and Huntington Riviera, on Huntington Drive through San Marino, and the Huntington Hotel and Huntington Hospital in Pasadena.

Moving to Los Angeles in 1902, he first lived in a hotel, then moved into the exclusive Jonathan Club, both downtown. He had left his family, the children grown, in San Francisco, and his marriage ended in divorce a few years later. In 1903 he purchased the 600-acre San Marino Ranch from the bank that had assumed ownership after the death of his friend James Shorb. There in a few years he would build a

An existing reservoir from the Shorb era had a fine collection of ducks among its waterfowl stock and a rustic bridge to a nesting island. Abandoned in 1925, it was filled in and became part of the cactus garden. This circa 1910 view shows the emerging cactus and palm gardens beyond and the mansion under construction on the hilltop to the left.

new house where the Shorb mansion stood, but the place had fallen on hard times and rethinking the landscaping was the first order of business.

Huntington was fortunate to find the German-born William Hertrich, whose professional experience had begun at age sixteen with a four-year apprenticeship in an Austrian firm. Immigrating to America in 1900, he eventually settled in California. In letters and in his book, *The Huntington Botanical Gardens, 1905–1949, Personal Recollections of William Hertrich,* he recounts the development of the estate and his working relationship with Henry Huntington.

The first tasks were to study the lay of the land, upgrade existing facilities, and install roads, irrigation, and fencing. Hertrich also established a nursery for grand-scale planting to come. Special gardens within the larger framework would follow in later years.

One of Huntington's landscaping tenets was to avoid formality where possible, except for several spaces designed later on to relate to the house and library. He considered his handsome native Engelmann and coast live oaks, of which perhaps a thousand still remain, an asset to be cherished. For preservation, some oaks were transplanted, and new planting had to respect the positions of those left in place.

In selecting plant material Huntington wanted to emphasize flowers for color in winter and early spring, the time of year when he intended his house to be

1921: An aerial view of the north section of the estate when it was still occupied by the Huntingtons. The 600-acre ranch was reduced to 207 acres when it became a public institution.

Today: The Huntington complex is an oasis of greenery in the midst of the sprawling metropolis

LEFT: A large domelike cage in the aviary's center housed twenty-six kinds of parrots and sixty-five other kinds of seed-eating birds. Built for Arabella Huntington, who was fond of birds and animals, the aviary had twelve sections for different special collections. It was torn down after her death.

RIGHT: Hertrich became an expert at transplanting large trees because Henry Huntington wanted the gardens to look mature as quickly as possible. These workers are transplanting a three-ton cactus, *Cereus alacriportanus*, in 1925.

occupied. The annual bloom calendar still shows the most kinds of plants flowering in February through April.

Proving to be a practical rancher, H. E. raised oranges as a cash crop. He started the first commercial avocado orchard in California with 300 seeds, many of them saved for him by the chef at the Jonathan Club in Los Angeles. Seeking practical information useful to a major land and rail developer, he collected trees, particularly palms, and other plants to test their adaptability to home gardens, parks, streets, and rail rights-of-way.

Since Huntington wanted his grounds to have an established look as quickly as possible, Hertrich looked for mature as well as rare specimens as he drove about with his horse and buggy, even on Sundays, cruising nurseries and other sources. He would truck in large trees from near and far, often under difficult conditions, and even brought three carloads of young saguaro cacti by train from Arizona.

Huntington and Hertrich would also travel together seeking plant material and lore at nurseries and other estates from San Diego to Santa Barbara. They visited some legendary plant specialists.

In 1904 the Sturtevant nursery in Hollywood supplied the water lilies, lotus,

This early view of the desert garden was photographed by William Hertrich, whose photo albums are an important source of documentation for the developing years of the estate.

and other aquatic plants for the first special garden at San Marino Ranch, a set of lily ponds started by his predecessor but completed by Hertrich. Two of the most specialized collections, palms and desert plants, began the next year. When Hertrich proposed the first, Huntington readily agreed, for palms were a personal favorite. They began bringing in species from the tropics and from places with temperate climates similar to that of San Marino to test their local performance, a procedure they would follow again and again when garden developments came up for consideration. Hertrich found many specimens in nearby nurseries, traveled east to find others, and had some sent from nurseries in Europe and Japan.

Huntington was less enthusiastic about desert plants, remembering a prickly encounter while supervising SP rail building in Arizona. Yet little-known desert plants seemed the only solution for a prominent area of poor soil that defied conventional greenery. At last the astute Hertrich won approval by appealing to his employer's collector instincts. A cactus and succulent collection evolved gradually from the few species Hertrich could find locally, augmented later with shipments from Arizona and Mexico. Eventually enlarged to twelve acres, the desert garden achieved such stature that some former competitors for specimens donated their

Rendering by architect
Elmer Grey, a partner of
Myron Hunt, of the house
for the Huntington estate.
The client eliminated
the proposed stairs and
terraces down the slope
south of the house, which
he thought too formal.

collections to the Huntington. In our time it shines as a star of the show.

Other installations followed. By 1909 a greenhouse for orchids and other tropicals had been built, a collection of camellias was underway, and a large collection of cycads was in place. A Japanese garden, now one of the most popular features of the estate, was completed in 1912.

With landscaping well along, the time came to build the house. Huntington selected the well-known architectural firm of Myron Hunt and Elmer Grey to design a stately new mansion in the Beaux Arts style on the site of Shorb's old Victorian house. After a year of construction the residence—today's Huntington Art Gallery—was completed in 1911. Its related outdoor spaces included an impressive loggia, a broad terrace, and two formal gardens—a rose garden to the west and the North Vista. This long grass allée, lined with a living colonnade of smooth palm trunks, focused on a baroque fountain backed by dramatic mountains beyond. Later on, Italian garden statuary added to the palms' architectural effect, and camellias and azaleas provided winter color.

BY 1910 HUNTINGTON had retired and put aside most business affairs to devote his time to art and book collecting. He already had a formidable reputation based

This Italian parterre is in the Dorothy Collins Brown Garden in front of the MaryLou and George Boone Gallery. Once the Huntingtons' garage designed by Myron Hunt, the building was adapted for re-use by Levin and Associates.

on his avid and increasingly knowledgeable pursuit of literary material, often buying rare manuscripts, volumes, and whole libraries at or even before auction. In time he would become America's foremost book collector. Eventually his holdings grew so great that he engaged Myron Hunt to design another major building, a library, on his estate grounds. Begun in 1919, it was completed the following year, though the interior would require several more years to finish.

In 1913 he married the widow of his uncle Collis, Arabella Duval Huntington, who was close to his age. One of America's wealthiest women, especially after Collis's legacy, she was also one of the important art collectors of her time. The newlyweds moved into their palatial new house in 1914. Until Arabella died in 1924 they divided their time between San Marino and their New York mansion, with an occasional stay in Europe.

Huntington was fully aware of the stature of his estate. In 1919 he assured its future with a trust indenture to create and fund the library, gallery, and gardens that would grow into today's institution, on 207 acres of the original premises. Before the ranch was reduced to that size, H. E. proudly pointed out that its production of citrus and other crops had made it self-supporting. The new boundaries preserved about 20 acres of orange groves along with the best of the ornamental plantings.

Banks of bright red *Rosa* 'Scarlet Meidiland' bloom in front of the Munger Research Center, which opened in 2004. The center houses rare book and manuscript collections, laboratories for conservation, photography, and digital imaging as well as research offices.

Huntington lived until 1927, spending most of his final years in San Marino. As the end neared, he had architect John Russell Pope design a mausoleum where he and Arabella would be interred. She had selected the site at the property's high point, in the northwest section by the orange groves. A prototype for Pope's future Jefferson Memorial in Washington, the chaste white marble structure was completed in 1929, after the death of its occupants.

In Huntington's lifetime the garden collections expanded through propagation, purchase, trading, and donation of plants, rootstock, and cuttings from nurserymen and other sources. Though funds for acquisition dropped after 1927, gifts continued, mainly because of William Hertrich's wide personal contact with plantsmen. Hertrich retired in 1948, but continued to watch over his beloved gardens until, frail at 88, he died in 1966.

WHEN HENRY HUNTINGTON passed away, less than half of the 207 acres had been developed as gardens. Today that figure has grown to about 120 acres landscaped and open to visitors.

The Lois and Robert F. Erburu Gallery, designed by architect Frederick Fisher, features a glass-enclosed loggia, enabling visitors to view the gardens and works of art at the same time.

Superintendent Hertrich's successor today is the director of the botanical gardens, one of the institution's major divisions. A staff for research, development, and maintenance includes curators in charge of separate garden areas and plant specialties. Collection and study of plants continue with such activities as field trips, exchange of seeds and plants, propagation, hybridizing, operation of a herbarium, and other activities.

These days the gardens have many distinctions: one of the world's foremost collections of cacti and other desert plants, one of America's largest collections of temperate-climate palms, the nation's largest collection of camellias, a garden of 1,200 kinds of roses grouped historically, a major Japanese garden, and many landmark, unusual, and rare plant specimens.

If Henry Huntington were to return, he likely would agree that the gardens contribute the kind of setting that one of the world's most important libraries and one of America's most important art collections deserve. The triad constitutes Southern California's premier showplace of the arts of civilization.

PLANT LANGUAGE

MOST BUT NOT ALL garden plants have common names, which may vary by region. Botanical names, consisting of a genus and species name, sometimes followed by a subspecies, variety, cultivar, or other designation, provide a more standardized terminology. Common names are not italicized, botanical names are in Latin and are italicized. The first word in a botanical name gives the genus (plural: genera), a major subdivision of a plant family that may contain one or many species distinct from one another but closely related. The second word gives the species, a further subdivision in classification. A third word may designate subspecies or variety, plants that share major characteristics with minor differences, or cultivar, a contraction of "cultivated variety" denoting a variety originated in cultivation. In abbreviations, "ssp." means subspecies, "spp." means species in the plural, "var." means variety. The lowest subdivision of a species is forma, abbreviated "f.," used to indicate a trivial variation such as a different color. A hybrid, the result of a cross between two genera, species, or varieties, is designated by an "x" between the names, as in *Coleus* x *hybridus*.

Thus the plant name Rosemary (*Rosmarinus officinalis* 'Lockwood de Forest') gives the common name, genus *Rosmarinus*, species *officinalis*, and cultivar name, 'Lockwood de Forest'. If another rosemary is mentioned immediately, the genus would be abbreviated "*R.*" followed by the species and variety.

Some other special terms: endemic, a plant native only to a particular location; epiphyte, a plant that grows without soil on another plant without receiving nourishment from it; exotic, often loosely equated to strange, in botanical usage it is reserved for plants of foreign or out-of-state origin; sport, considered a mutation, a plant whose leaves or flowers vary spontaneously from the normal; xerophyte, a plant adapted to arid conditions; hardy, resistant to frost, and tender, not resistant to frost; succulent, a plant that stores water and nutrients in leaves, stem, or roots.

Strelitzia juncea flowers resemble the more commonly cultivated bird of paradise (*Strelitzia reginae*).

Australian Garden

Conifer Collection

Lily Ponds

Subtropical Garden

Desert Garden

Jungle Garden

Huntington Gallery

North

Palm Garden

Library

Munger Research Center

Map by Lisa Pompelli

This map plots the public area of the gardens, which cover about 120 acres; the rest of the property is undeveloped and not open to the public.

· THE HUNTINGTON ·
LIBRARY, ART COLLECTIONS, BOTANICAL GARDENS

Japanese Garden

North Canyon (camellias)

Rose Garden

Herb Garden

Boone Gallery

Future Chinese Garden

kespeare den

Dorothy Collins Brown Garden

Erburu Gallery

Scott Gallery

Associated Foundations Teaching Greenhouse

Rose Hills Foundation Conservatory for Botanical Science

Helen and Peter Bing Children's Garden

Mausoleum

In The Gardens, Part I

THE EARLY GARDENS

· THE LILY PONDS ·
OLDEST OF THE SPECIALTY GARDENS

A black-crowned night heron is among the many birds visiting the lily ponds.

LEFT: Water lilies bloom in summer.

PAGES 32–33: The path to the desert garden is fringed by *Agave attenuata* 'Boutin Blue' and *Aloe barberae*, first planted around 1950.

HENRY HUNTINGTON began his first themed garden in 1904, a set of half a dozen lily ponds installed for the practical purpose of replacing a shallow, unsightly gully in the southeast corner of the gardens with something more presentable. To complete the project, begun by his predecessor before he was fired, William Hertrich devised an innovative warm-water system—later abandoned—for one pond that kept such species as the giant water lily *Victoria amazonica* in bloom well into winter. Appropriately, here where it all started a plaque now memorializes Hertrich as the botanical gardens' innovative designer and developer.

Around the ponds several acres without visible boundaries present a vision of Elysian fields, matured over the years into a display of water lilies, lotus, and other aquatic plants in a sylvan setting of bamboo groves, lawn, and tall trees. A cascading stream down from an adjacent jungle garden enhances the scene and through aeration contributes to water quality. The ponds are home to bright-colored koi (Japanese carp), turtles, frogs, and resident and visiting ducks.

Descendants of a long history of water lily (*Nymphaea*) cultivation are seen in the ponds, where many varieties grow in profusion and blossom in varied hues mid-spring through mid-autumn. Their magnificent relative, the sacred or East Indian lotus (*Nelumbo nucifera*), dominates one of the lower ponds, where some of the original plants remain from their introduction in 1905. In summer they lift impressive pink and white flowers eight or nine inches across on stems above inverted-parasol leaves fourteen or more inches across.

A 1916 view of one of the lily ponds with the mansion at the top of the hill.

OPPOSITE: The sacred lotus (*Nelumbo nucifera*) unfurls immense, pink-tipped petals above broad upturned umbrella leaves. The flower color of lotus ranges from white through shades of pink.

Along the shoreline cannas, strelitzias, and cordyline contribute bold leaf patterns, and the water-loving papyrus (*Cyperus papyrus*) adds grace. The bulrush of the Bible, this tall sedge used for making writing paper in the ancient world grows along the Nile from Egypt south into Uganda.

Close by across a stretch of lawn west of the ponds, the Huntington's unusual conifer collection was planted in this cool spot to favor species from temperate areas. The grove holds several araucarias, Southern Hemisphere natives whose common names include the word "pine," though true pines all come from the Northern Hemisphere. The best-known here is Norfolk Island pine (*Araucaria heterophylla*) and there are specimens of New Caledonia pine (*A. columnaris*) and hoop pine (*A. cunninghamii*). An unusual pine relative, *Keteleeria evelyniana*, comes from China. Two are cypress relatives, Taiwan redwood (*Taiwania cryptomerioides*) from Taiwan and Montezuma cypress (*Taxodium mucronatum*) from Mexico. Two are so-called living fossils from that ancient time before flowering plants evolved, the dawn redwood (*Metasequoia glyptostroboides*), a deciduous conifer thought to be extinct until it was discovered growing in China in 1948, and the deciduous maidenhair tree (*Ginkgo biloba*), related to the conifers and extremely rare in the wild.

Among notable non-conifers growing nearby are such flowering trees as strawberry snowball (*Dombeya cacuminum*) from Madagascar, sweetshade (*Hymenosporum flavum*) from Australia, the largest southern magnolia (*Magnolia grandiflora*) specimen on the grounds—and a specimen of a commercially important food plant from Australia, *Macadamia integrifolia*, beloved by resident squirrels for its late-summer bounty of nuts.

· THE BAMBOO COLLECTION ·
THE GIANT GRASSES, LARGE AND SMALL

MORE THAN SEVENTY-FIVE species of these giant grasses grow near the lily ponds, in the jungle and Japanese gardens, and along the edges of the public parking lot. Most are of the clump-forming *Bambusa* genus, indigenous to subtropical areas, whose rhizomes or underground stems grow out only a short distance before sending up new vertical stems called culms. On the north side of the ponds are plantings of *Himalayacalamus porcatus,* distinguished by its blue culms, *Thamnocalamus spathiflorus* var. *crassinoides* with red culms, and *Dendrocalamus brandisii,* native of India, which has the tallest culms in the world, reaching 100 feet in its natural surroundings.

The temperate bamboos, those that grow in colder regions of the world, such as the running *Phyllostachys* genus, have rhizomes that grow underground for greater distances before sending up new culms.

A stand of punting-pole bamboo (*Bambusa tuldoides*), tallest of the clumping bamboos, is prominent just west of the lower lily ponds. Among the ponds, dense groves meet overhead to create shady tunnels over water and pathways. These are *B. glaucescens, B. tuldoides,* and *B. oldhamii,* bamboo specimens planted in 1906 as some of Henry Huntington's first garden acquisitions. Isolated in the lawn near the middle pond is a large stately 100-year-old clump of *B. beecheyana,* whose emerging culms are clothed in bright orange sheaths. North of the ponds is a clump of Buddha's belly bamboo (*B. ventricosa*), a curiosity that under drought stress produces inflated internodes on the lower sections of bamboo canes that suggest the ample belly of Buddha statues.

In the jungle garden by the waterfall is a tropical timber bamboo, *Dendrocalamus asper* from south Asia. It has dense tan fuzz on young culms, handsome foliage, and can grow fifty feet tall. Close to the jungle garden's eastern edge grows one of the small clumping bamboos of the American tropics, *Chusquea coronalis,* whose long delicate green plumes grow like a vine.

Temperate bamboos grow in the Japanese garden, including luxuriant stands of golden or fishpole bamboo (*Phyllostachys aurea*), one of the best kinds for edible shoots, which line both sides of the south or lower entrance. Two others nearby are black bamboo (*P. nigra*), named for its mottled culms turning a solid black in maturity under a mass of short, light green leaves, and the large timber bamboo *P. vivax.* On the bank near the road, *Pleioblastus chino* 'Variegatus,' a low-growing groundcover, shows off its green foliage striped bright yellow. On the opposite bank, approaching the Japanese house, is another low growing, running bamboo, *P. argenteostriatus* 'Albostriatus', with its green leaves variegated white.

OPPOSITE: A large grove of bamboo creates a cool dimness in the lower part of the Japanese garden. Seen here on the left is *Phyllostachys aurea* and on the right, *P. nigra* 'Punctata'.

New spring shoots of giant timber bamboo (*Phyllostachys vivax*) poke up through a mulch of its own leaves in the Japanese garden.

OPPOSITE: An impenetrable stand of golden bamboo (*Phyllostachys aurea*), its slender stems topped by a cascade of pale green, guards the south entrance to the Japanese garden.

· THE PALM GARDEN ·
ICONS OF TROPICAL CLIMES

Huntington's first collection garden, devoted to palms, tested many tropical species that did not survive severe winter frosts. Today the emphasis is on temperate-climate palms. The pleated leaves of a low-growing, widely branching Mediterranean fan palm (*Chamaerops humilis*), the only palm native to Europe, sweep the ground, revealing the dense panicles of yellow flowers at its heart.

The fruit and flower clusters of the solitary fishtail palm (*Caryota urens*) can grow ten feet long.

BEYOND THE LAWN south of the entrance pavilion a grove of palms, now dense, now more open, creates one of the Huntington's most remarkable landscapes. Here four acres of the most decorative and botanically interesting temperate-climate palms form the nucleus of a continually enlarging collection of over two hundred species.

Palms were favorite trees of Henry Huntington's, by themselves and as landscaping subjects in gardens and public places and along streets and rail routes. Indeed they were immensely popular in Southern California of the Golden Age for their evocation of the tropics and the romance of faraway places. Some species also came to be known as the most architectural of trees, in lines along stately avenues and in formal landscaping. In time the palm became the region's signature tree.

Begun in 1905, the Huntington collection grew quickly with many large specimens and many tropical species. The tender species provided the kind of knowledge expected from test plantings: they perished in frosts that occurred once each decade from 1913 to 1949. It became evident that not all palms that thrive close to the coast are hardy in the San Gabriel Valley's colder winters, yet some early-day veterans remain and new introductions are being tried, mostly in a warm micro-climate shared with the adjacent jungle garden (page 141).

Outside the palm garden, Guadalupe Island palms (*Brahea edulis*) line Palm Drive on the way to the mausoleum. Their handsome, regular crowns and stature make them useful avenue trees.

A walk through this small forest reveals a strong family resemblance among palms, a close look turns up striking variations. Most have single upright, unbranched trunks but some have multiple trunks. Most have fan-shaped or feathery leaves atop their trunks but some have undivided leaves and some grow fronds close to the ground. Some reach great height, a few are small. And though most palms prefer the tropics and subtropics, some grow in colder latitudes. Here are a few of special interest:

The Mediterranean fan palm (*Chamaerops humilis*), the only one native to Europe, gave palms their name. Noting a resemblance to the human hand's palm and fingers, the Romans called the tree palma, the Latin root of the English word.

The Chilean wine palm (*Jubaea chilensis*), endemic to the valley of Ocoa in central Chile, is the most massive of the palms, with a three-foot-thick trunk that resembles a stocky column from an early Greek temple. It is prized for its sugary sap, which ferments into a crude wine that can be extracted only after the tree is felled, so many trees in native stands have been lost and the species is endangered.

Remaining from a planting along the estate's former main access road are South American jelly palms (*Butia capitata*), with stout trunks and feathery, gray-green leaves. In the fall hundreds of their edible yellow or orange fruits dot the lawn.

Several of the date palm genus *Phoenix* adapt well here. The familiar Canary Island date palm (*P. canariensis*) is California's most widely planted large street

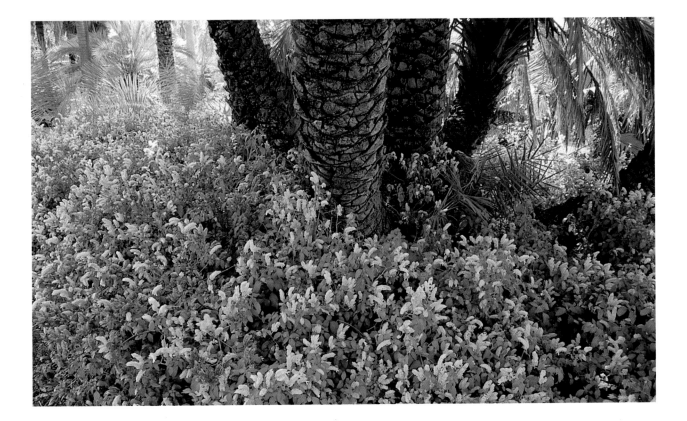

This clump of trunks belongs to the date palm (*Phoenix dactylifera*), which is usually grown commercially as a single-trunk tree. Shrimp plant (*Justicia brandegeana* 'Chartreuse') surrounds the palms with color.

and garden palm. A stately specimen in the nearby desert garden was shipped by Henry Huntington from his uncle Collis P. Huntington's house in San Francisco, destroyed in the 1906 earthquake and fire. The date palm (*P. dactylifera*) also grows here, but bears fruit only in hot desert locations. The cliff date palm (*P. rupicola*), from rugged places in the Himalayas, including the Indian states of Sikkim and Assam, is represented by three specimens twenty-five feet tall, with slender trunks and bright green leafy crowns.

The Canary Island date palm is magnificent for its imposing mature height (to sixty feet) and spread of its crown (to fifty feet). The majesty palm (*Ravenea rivularis*) merits its common name for its perfection of form. Several windmill palms from the Himalayas, *Trachycarpus martianus*, are the most mature specimens on public display in Southern California.

Eleven species of the fan palm genus *Brahea* from Mexico and one from Central America grow in the garden, many of them grown from seed collected south of the border. From Baja California come the tallest braheas, San Jose hesper palm (*B. brandegeei*), and the blue hesper palm (*B. armata*). The Guadalupe Island palm (*B. edulis*) is endemic to the island of that name 160 miles off the Mexican coast. Other species range variously from Sonora and elsewhere in Mexico, while *B. salvadorensis* is from Central America.

Two other fan palms grow in both the palm and desert gardens. California fan palm (*Washingtonia filifera*) and the Mexican fan palm (*W. robusta*) are found

The massive gray trunk of the Chilean wine palm (*Jubaea chilensis*) is topped with stiff featherlike foliage, dull green above and grayish beneath.

OPPOSITE: Senegal date palms (*Phoenix reclinata*) frame a bench placed for a view of the lower part of the palm garden.

in desert oases with springs and underground water. The Mexican species was widely planted in Southern California long before anyone realized it would grow so tall and out of scale on city streets that the irreverent would call it a "telephone pole with a fright wig"—useful if unkind horticultural information.

The palmettos, genus *Sabal*, are all from the Americas. Cabbage palmetto (*S. palmetto*), native from South Carolina to Florida, Cuba, and the Bahamas, has a trunk twenty to ninety feet tall, edible fruit, wood for building, and leaves for roof thatching, baskets, mats, and hats. The Texas palmetto (*S. mexicana*), native from Texas to Guatemala, has a stockier trunk, and the dwarf species *S. minor*, native from Georgia to Florida and Texas, has a six-foot or shorter trunk.

The so-called saw palmetto, not a sabal but *Serenoa repens*, may derive its common name from a shared habitat with the sabals and a resemblance to *Sabal minor.* Slow-growing, often in a dense knee-high scrub, it is native from South Carolina to the Florida Keys and coastal Texas.

One of two Asian fishtail palms, *Caryota ochlandra*, from southern China, is seen in the palm garden. The other, *C. urens*, from south Asia, is in the jungle garden nearby. These handsome, fast-growing trees have a life span of only about twenty years, producing inflorescences or flower clusters only in their final years.

Fine examples of Senegal date palm (*Phoenix reclinata*) stand out near the entrance pavilion. Several palms contribute to the Huntington Gallery landscaping, among them, one of the tenderest of all, an unidentified species of royal palm (*Roystonea*) from the Caribbean. Other palms are planted in the North Vista, along Palm Drive in the north part of the gardens, and along Euston Road, bordering the gardens on the south.

Above: Tall California fan palms (*Washingtonia filifera*), the sole palm native to California, dominate the skyline of the desert garden. The Canary Island date palm *(Phoenix canariensis)* in the middle of this picture was moved from Collis Huntington's house in San Francisco to San Marino Ranch.

Left: Here behind the short form of the multi-trunked *Chamaerops humilis* is the typical form of this palm. The Canary Island date palm, the most widely planted large palm in California, is at right.

· THE DESERT GARDEN ·
PLANTS FROM EXTREME ENVIRONMENTS

Spiny plants are close to the walkways in the desert garden, tempting visitors to touch at their peril. Seen here are saguaro cactus at left overlooking the much smaller golden barrel cactus. Red-flowering aloes and yucca's white flowers brighten the scene.

Golden barrel cacti (*Echinocactus grusonii*) are seen in the small picture at right.

A T FIRST, PEOPLE unfamiliar with the planet's arid regions are likely to find the desert garden's plants bizarre. Then, like anyone who has been beguiled by the austere beauties of such places as Baja California, the deserts of mainland Mexico, Africa, or our own Desert Southwest, they discover the collection to be an endless delight. The garden displays, as few others anywhere do, a rich variety of plants of bold geometric and sculptural shapes, strong textures, and some of nature's most dazzling color in flower and leaf. Equally important, it reveals the astonishing ways by which desert plants cope with drought and defend themselves against enemies. The garden distinguishes Henry Huntington as a great collector for bringing together a major plant group largely unknown and little appreciated in his time, when deserts were widely thought to be wastelands of little value.

Begun as a cactus garden and later expanded to the broader category of succulents and xerophytes, the desert garden grew to preeminence and today remains one of the world's finest. It has also become one of the Huntington's most botanically important gardens. Many

Young leaves at the core of the bromeliad popularly called heart of flame (*Bromelia balansae*) turn a brilliant red before the plant flowers in late spring. This member of the pineapple family has thorny leaves and a tight growth habit to ward off herbivores.

of its specimens, grown over the years to unusual size, are now all the more valuable for science and education because curators have precise records of their origin and growth. Today the garden and a conservatory, to be noted presently, contain more than five thousand species, half the plants in the world considered to be succulent —that is, plants that store water in leaf, stem, or root.

More than a showcase, the garden also functions as a laboratory for the study of physical properties of plants and their adaptations to growing conditions. It is also a place where new plants can be tested for landscape value, selected, hybridized, and propagated for introduction to the horticultural trade.

It can also supply material for research on desert plants for food, pharmacology, and industrial uses, continuing an age-old pursuit. As a sampling, *Aloe vera* produces a healing, cosmetic agent; the dragon tree (*Dracaena draco*) exudes a red "dragon's blood" resin used as a violin wood preservative in Italy; euphorbias yield products for such varied uses as commercial waxes and rubber and poisons for catching fish or tipping arrows; jojoba (*Simmondsia chinensis*) yields an oil for high-tech uses to replace sperm whale oil. Many plants have had multiple uses. Early peoples in Mexico used agaves, for example, for food from edible root crowns and flower stalks; as fiber for fabric, paper, thread, and cordage; and for alcoholic drinks fermented from stem sap to make pulque, in turn distilled to make tequilas and mescals. In our time agaves produce material for formulating such useful drugs as cortisone and the hormones estrogen and progesterone.

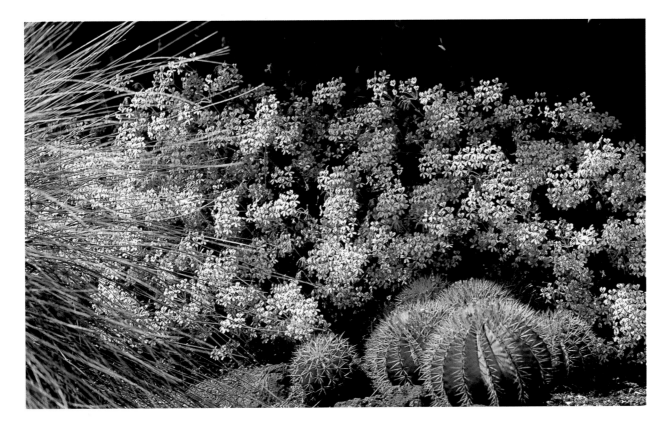

Blossoms of *Pelargonium echinatum* range in color from white to pink and dark purple.

The garden was not created to imitate desert scenes but rather to explore botanical, horticultural, and landscaping aspects of xerophytes from the world over. It began in 1907, when William Hertrich persuaded Henry Huntington to try cacti in an area of poor soil that resisted conventional planting. Though reluctant because of a previous personal encounter with cactus spines, Huntington agreed to an experiment on half an acre, and Hertrich gradually moved in some three hundred cacti. That included a mature *Cereus xanthocarpus*, old when installed and now one of the garden's oldest and most massive cactus. In 1908 Hertrich brought back from Arizona three carloads of saguaro (*Carnegiea gigantea*) and other cacti. In 1912 he brought two carloads of cacti and other succulents from Mexico. That year the garden expanded to five acres and in 1925 it acquired five more acres on fill over a former irrigation reservoir. Specimens of *Yucca filifera*, the tallest yucca, still remain from plantings around the shore, an irregular line of venerable trees through the lower garden. Beginning in 1929 Hertrich planted a bank of pincushion cacti (*Mammillaria*) beside the central path in more than a thousand linear feet of scoria, a porous red basalt, a planting destined for fame decades later as one of the world's premier rockeries. After a lull during the Depression and World War II, momentum resumed in the 1960s, with the garden's scope enlarged to include many newly discovered species from arid lands around the world. In 1981 the area grew to its present ten acres, and in 1985 a desert garden conservatory opened to the public.

The garden has sixty plant beds, numbered for identification, some of them

The central part of the garden displays a medley of cacti, especially
a large collection of golden barrels (*Echinocactus grusonii*).

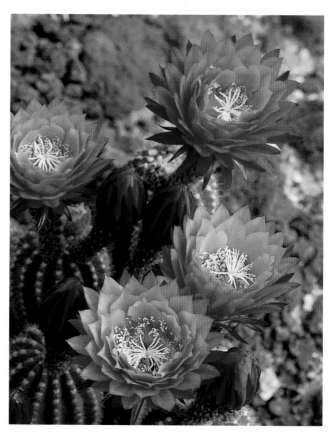

TOP LEFT: Pink flowers of *Echinopsis* 'Stars and Stripes'

TOP RIGHT: Many colorful *Echinopsis* hybrids are displayed in the lower garden. Usually they flower from April through June and are winter hardy. The *Trichocereus* group has taller, ribbed stems and equally vibrant flowers.

BOTTOM LEFT: Seed capsules of *Cheiridopsis roodiae*, reminiscent of passion flower, open to release their cargo for germination.

BOTTOM RIGHT: The tiny yellow flowers of the crown of thorns euphorbia (*Euphorbia milii* var. *splendens*) lack petals but are encircled by showy red bracts.

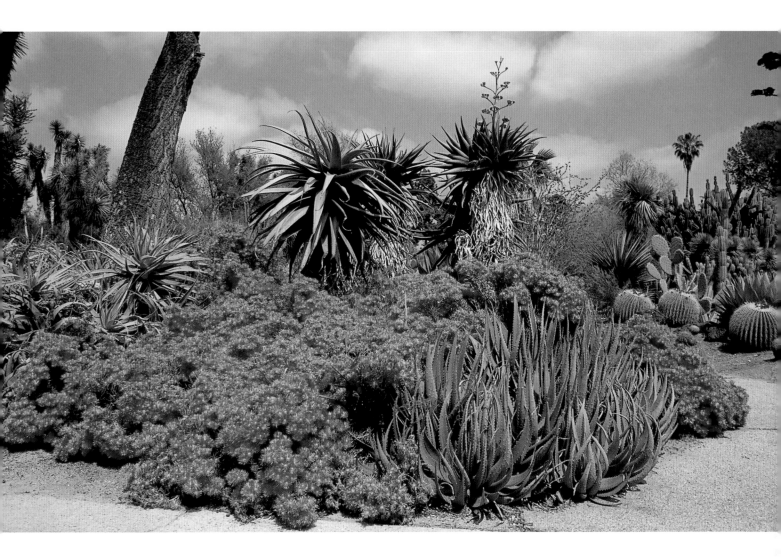

This panoramic view features the spectacular magenta-flowered *Lampranthus amoenus*, blooming February to March. The aloe in the foreground is a hybrid of *Aloe aculeata*; the aloes in the left background are *A. pluridens* crosses, and in the center background is *A. ferox* x *A. microstigma*.

with two or more subdivisions. It straddles the same south-facing fault scarp that benefits other botanical garden segments with a sunny slope and a cold-air flow that on frosty nights can produce a critical temperature differential of five degrees between upper and lower reaches. The northern high ground is devoted mostly to the Old World, the western and southwestern parts of the garden to North America, and the low southeastern part to South America, plus numerous plantings native to both Old and New Worlds.

Most specimens have been planted where they will grow best, but some beds do represent regional flora. The first, Baja California, was followed by beds devoted to the Sonoran and Chihuahuan deserts of Mexico and our Southwest, California deserts, various South American regions, and Madagascar.

Let us look now at a few garden highlights, proceeding roughly from high to low and north to south.

Near the conservatory in the upper section, home to South African succulents,

ABOVE LEFT: A flowering branch of *Puya coerulea* var. *violacea*, native to Chile, as it appears in April to May. Much of the color of this puya's blooms is derived from the reddish stalks. The similarly colored bracts nearly conceal the almost-black flowers, which grow high above what seems an unpromising clump of spiky grass.

ABOVE RIGHT: The xerophytic bromeliad *Puya venusta*, also from Chile, forms impenetrable thickets of tightly clumped, silver-leaved rosettes. In spring, it produces pink-bracted, scepter-like inflorescences that bear rings of violet flowers.

are found treelike euphorbia species that resemble columnar cacti seen elsewhere in the garden. Nearly all cacti are native to the Americas, so the comparison makes a graphic example of convergent evolution, in which unrelated plants have evolved similar adaptations to similar environments in different locations. Nearby, the small milk barrel euphorbia (*Euphorbia horrida*) likewise resembles a barrel cactus. Flower size offers one way to distinguish between look-alike euphorbias and cacti: those of euphorbias are usually small and inconspicuous, those of the cacti are typically large and showy.

In the same area, the crown of thorns euphorbia (*E. milii* var. *hislopii*), native to Madagascar, shares its common name with a species more likely to be the one mentioned in the Bible: the thorny tree *Ziziphus spina-christi*, planted behind the euphorbia.

Two hundred species of aloe throughout the upper garden stage the Huntington's most exuberant color spectacle in winter with flower clusters of brilliant red, orange, and yellow. Mostly from South Africa, some aloes are stemless, some are trees, all are leaf succulent—that is, they store moisture in their leaves. Near the conservatory, a grove of giant tree aloe (*Aloe barberae,* also known as *A. bainesii*) specimens stands out; tallest of the aloes, they can reach fifty feet in their native habitat.

Near them is one of the most useful of the genus *Agave* for landscaping, the gray-green *A. attenuata*. Planted close to it is a unique blue variant, *A. attenuata* 'Boutin Blue', brought back from Mexico in 1970 by a Huntington team, which shows promise as a garden subject. The desert garden contains nearly half of the two hundred known agave species. Most are mistakenly called century plants because

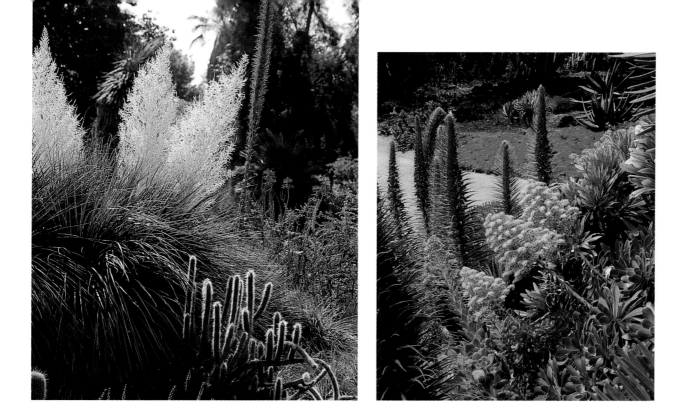

of the long interval before they put out flower stalks, but that period is more like seven to thirty-five years than a hundred. Spectacular and as tall as thirty feet, those stalks spring from basal leaf clusters called rosettes, which may be a few inches to fifteen feet high, depending on the species. Agaves range from the southern United States to northern South America; most come from Mexico.

A specimen of special interest is an *Agave celsii* var. *albicans* in the Sonoran bed near the garden's lower entrance. It is listed as No. 1 in the botanical gardens' inventory register, begun in 1932—a list that by 2005 had passed 93,000 entries.

Crassulas, echeverias, kalanchoes, sedums, and other members of the crassula family spread varied colors of foliage and flower across the garden. One of the most unusual is a black aeonium (*Aeonium arboreum* 'Zwartkop'), dramatic with dark purple, almost black leaves ("zwartkop" means "black head" in Dutch).

One of the desert garden's most spectacular beds contains numerous pincushion cacti (*Mammillaria*) from Mexico. The two outstanding ones are *M. compressa*, forming mats that creep over the rocks, and *M. geminispina,* snow-white and mounding, suggesting a bubbling cascade as surely as white pebbles do in a skillfully executed Japanese dry-garden watercourse. In the same location, the golden barrel cactus (*Echinocactus grusonii*), a familiar desert plant, creates one of the garden's most dramatic landscape features for its numbers, form, and color. To cope with periods of drought it has accordionlike ribs that let the body expand as it stores water and contract as it uses it. Many of these slow-growing cacti, in place since 1925, weigh several hundred pounds when their moisture content is high.

Nearby is a striking example of a caudiciform, a term that refers to a water-and

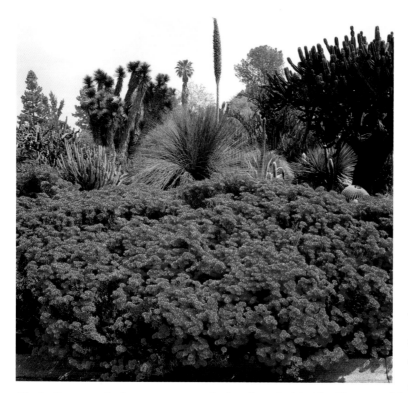

The brilliant purple daisy flowers of *Lampranthus amoenus,* one of the taller-growing species in the ice plant family, open at mid-day in early spring. Above rises the unmistakable spike of sotol.

OPPOSITE: In the Baja California planting bed, creeping devil (*Stenocereus eruca*) grows spiny stem segments that spread across the ground to form a spectacular ever-expanding patch, intimidating to intruders.

nutrient-storage organ in the stem or the root, either above or below ground level. It is the Mexican *Beaucarnea recurvata,* with a distended base to its scaly trunk, planted in impressive groves along the central path and the west edge of the garden. Not far away is a large specimen of the related *Nolina matapensis,* from the Mexican state of Sonora, with its crown of thick, grass-like leaves.

In the Baja California bed, the boojum tree or cirio (*Fouquieria columnaris*) is arguably Baja California's most unusual tree. Its erect, tapering trunk will bristle briefly with tiny leaves after a rain and it may sprout branches of unpredictable form at the apex. Here planted in a grove, it evokes Lewis Carroll's fantasy creature, the boojum, in his *The Hunting of the Snark.* Its other name, cirio, is from the Spanish for taper, referring to its candle shape. Cirio is related to the red-flowered ocotillo (*F. splendens*) of the southwestern deserts, and Adam's tree or palo adán (*F. diguetii*) from Sonora and Baja California, also seen here. The Baja California bed also has agaves, nolinas, dudleyas (*Dudleya brittonii*), and such cacti as cardon (*Pachycereus pringlei*), pitahaya agria (*Stenocereus gummosus*), and the remarkable creeping devil (*S. eruca*), a prostrate species that produces extensive spiny carpets.

An interesting prickly pear cactus is *Opuntia ellisiana* from Mexico, with flattened padlike stems on which the scale insect cochineal feeds; when dried and ground the insects produce a red fabric dye. Prickly-pear opuntias have succulent, padlike stems that function as leaves. Fruits of opuntias are edible and in some species the pad, the *nopal* of Mexico, is also eaten cooked as a vegetable.

The California desert bed illuminates the meaning of "exotic" as a plant that is native somewhere else. The Joshua tree (*Yucca brevifolia*), native to the Mojave Desert thirty miles north across the mountains, is exotic in San Marino and does

not fare well here. Our Lord's Candle (*Y. whipplei*), native to the San Gabriel and coastal mountains, occasionally appears in the garden.

Likewise exotic here are plants from the low desert a hundred miles away. An example of a tree from the desert but not a xerophyte is the California fan palm (*Washingtonia filifera*). It grows in oases in California, western Arizona, and northern Mexico that have water from springs, an underground stream, or a high water table. The related Mexican fan palm (*W. robusta*) occupies similar habitat from the border to much farther south, and despite its name, is the more slender of the two. Other plants in the California bed include brittlebush (*Encelia farinosa*), creosote bush (*Larrea tridentata*), and beavertail cactus (*Opuntia basilaris*).

Planted in several lower-garden beds, two rare xerophytic bromeliads, related to the pineapple, come from Chile. They bloom in the spring, *Puya alpestris* with flowers of ethereal blue-green, and *P. chilensis* with vivid chartreuse flowers. Both have hooked spined leaves with sawlike edges. Beside the main path in the middle of the garden another member of the pineapple family, *Abromeitiella brevifolia*, is seen clambering over the rocks in a giant mound.

In 2003 two acres in the garden's southeastern portion were relandscaped to create the Heritage Walk, offering a view of the landscape as it might have looked between 1907 and 1927, when the Huntington was a ranch and estate garden. On the hill are the remains of some stone steps laid by Hertrich in 1907, when he was ranch foreman. A portion of the walk contains the T. Harper Goodspeed puya collection obtained in the early 1930s.

Top left: Creamy flower clusters of *Yucca filifera* dangle from angled branches with a top-knot of bladelike leaves.

Top right: Part of the garden's showiest color is the winter flowering of two hundred species of aloe. Various hybrids are growing beneath a towering dragon tree.

Lower left: The distinctive red-orange and yellow poker-shaped inflorescences of *Aloe africana* are borne on short stems.

Lower right: The young leaves of *Agave nelsonii* retain the imprint of their nascent thorns.

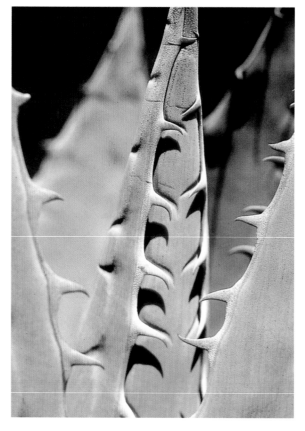

Opposite: Aloes range in size from the small single rosettes of *Aloe humilis* to *Aloe* 'Rooikappie', seen in the foreground, to the gracefully branched tree aloe (*A. barberae* or *A. bainesii*), tallest of the aloes. The succulent swordlike leaves of aloes are similar to those of agaves, but they do not die down after the plant has flowered.

· THE DESERT GARDEN CONSERVATORY ·
SHELTER FOR THE FRAGILE AND DELICATE

Welwitschia mirabilis, or marvelous welwitschia, has only two leaves, but they may live for more than a thousand years.

THE DESERT GARDEN is limited to plants that can grow in the San Gabriel Valley climate. The Desert Garden Conservatory, a greenhouse at the upper end of the garden, broadens the possible range of plants in the collection by providing the kind of shelter perhaps half of the world's succulent plants need to thrive here or even survive. Opened in 1985 for public viewing, it holds some 3,000 specimens under controlled conditions of temperature and irrigation and protected from trampling as well as competition by more vigorous plants.

Its specimens are grown in special unglazed stoneware pots in a potting mix designed for rapid drainage, with a top dressing to suppress weed and algal growth. Keeping out birds and insects protects plants from unwanted hybridization; so does hand pollination, done with small paint brushes. One conservatory activity, propagating and distributing rare species, reduces demand among collectors for plants from the wild, helping to preserve them in nature.

The conservatory's display is laid out on seven benches and a landscaped bed at the west end, while containers for large specimens are placed on the floor near the center. More than thirty-five plant families represented in the collection include the seven major families, which comprise seventy percent of all succulent species, and some of the more obscure. New World plants are grouped mostly south of the center aisle and Old World plants—from Europe, Africa, and Asia—are north of it and in the planting bed. Cacti are mostly on the south side, because they are native to the New World. The exception, *Rhipsalis baccifera,* found throughout the Old World and New World tropics, is displayed along with other epiphytic cacti on the north side.

Many are the curiosities to be seen here. Among them are plants that grow almost entirely underground except for their leaf tips, getting light to the interior with so-called windows in the tips. The lithops, "living stones," bear no resemblance to any other kind of plant; all that is visible are fleshy leaves that mimic the shape

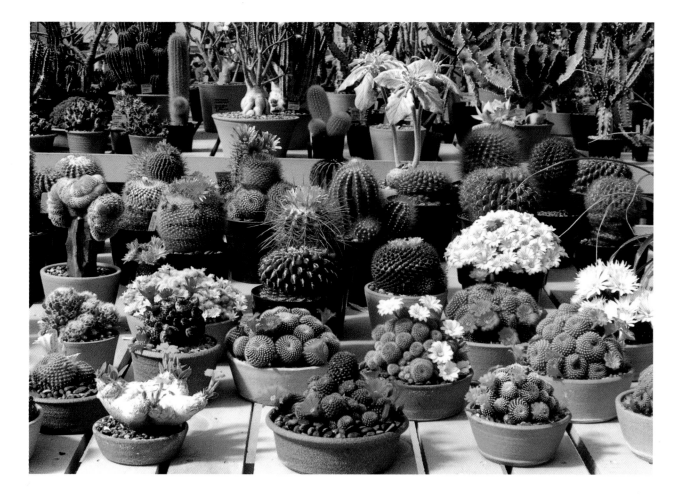

Some of the thirty-five plant families represented in the conservatory are shown in the picture above. Specimens are grown in stoneware pots in special potting mix.

RIGHT: The jewel flower of Mexico (*Tacitus bellus*) was discovered and introduced into cultivation in the early 1970s. It is part of the Huntington's extensive research collection of New World Crassulaceae, the crassula or stonecrop family.

and color of rocks or soil in their native habitat. Another mimicry adaptation comes from the *Ariocarpus*, cacti that avoid being eaten by resembling jagged stones. Perhaps the most remarkable of all the plants here is *Welwitschia mirabilis*, from the rainless desert of Namibia and Angola. It can live for more than a thousand years with only its original two leaves, which eventually grow to ten feet long on a trunk several feet wide but less than a foot high. A distant relative of the conifers and cycads, it produces seed from cones, not flowers. The largest plants here, started from seed in 1970, produced cones and seed only after fourteen years.

The planting bed at the west end features large Old World succulents. Prominent here are ten of the eleven species of Didiereaceae, a small family of succulent shrubs endemic to Madagascar, with sprawling, thorny stems that resemble those of the unrelated native of southwestern U.S. deserts, the ocotillo.

Opposite is a sampling of sta- peliad flowers, succulents in the milkweed family: *Orbea rogersii,* top left, with delicate glasslike hairs in the flower and an unpleasant scent; *Stape- lia flavopurpurea,* top right, with sweetly scented flowers; *Orbea semota,* bottom right, with brilliant yellow flowers and delicate hairs that flicker in the faintest breeze, perhaps as an attraction to pollinators; and *Huernia nouhuysii,* bottom left, with no fragance at all.

Lithops, this page top, the "living rocks", put out flowers from fissures across the middle. Many small, globular stemmed species of cacti, center row, make ideal container specimens: *Notocactus graessneri* var. *albisetus,* left, of Brazil is unusual for its bright green flowers. *Borzicactus weber- baueri,* center, of Peru has showy tubular flowers pollinated by hummingbirds. *Mammillaria pilcayensis,* right, is one of a genus of more than 150 species collec- tively known as pincushion cacti. *Rhipsalis boliviana,* bottom, collected on a Hun- tington expedition to Bolivia in 1984, is part of the Huntington's extensive research collection of epiphytic cacti.

IN THE GARDENS, PART II

THE MANSION AND
ESTATE GARDENS

· THE HUNTINGTON GALLERY GARDEN ·
LANDSCAPING AROUND A MANSION

This plant screen on the north and east side of the loggia was intended to create a partial enclosure so the space could be used as an outdoor room.

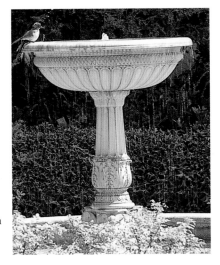

PAGES 70–71: Late afternoon shadows on the Library lawn

THE MANSION, now the Huntington Art Gallery, occupies the heart of the most intensively developed portion of the gardens. Seen from its south terrace, the property's grand estate scale is still apparent in expansive views across lawns on three sides. To the east, the prospect reaches to the entrance and palm gardens. A broad crescent formed by tall-tree boundaries of the jungle and subtropical gardens extends southeast to southwest as far as the rose garden west of the house. North of the house the landscape elements are closer together: a circle formed by a porte-cochere entry road, the stately North Vista and its flanking camellia gardens, and the Shakespeare garden.

As founder Huntington intended, the gardens—even when large-scale and formal—retain a so-called softscape character, that is, plants are more important in landscaping than structure. Plants create the setting for the mansion, rather than such architectural extensions proposed by architect Myron Hunt, but not accepted by Huntington, as balustraded terraces down the slope from the south terrace. Even the North Vista's formal elements

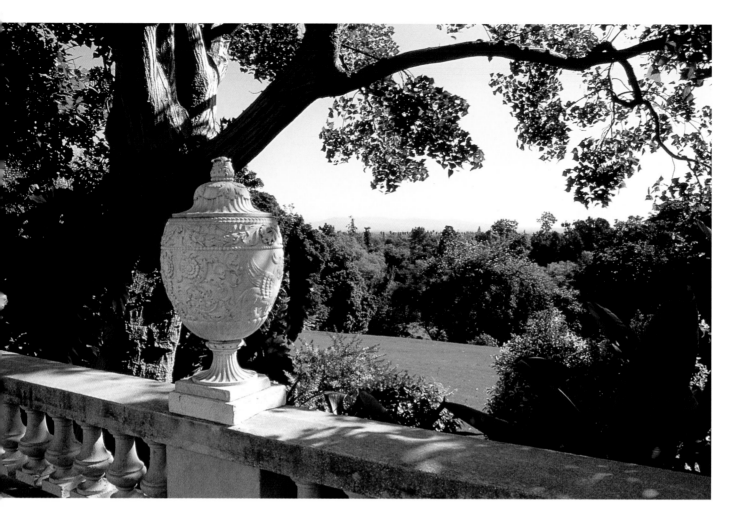

In the view from the mansion's south terrace, a long line of mature trees in the subtropical and jungle gardens screens off the intensively urbanized San Gabriel Valley. The terrace surveyed a rural scene in the first decades of the last century, when the house was new.

OPPOSITE: In winter, blooming *Erythrina caffra* frames the east entrance to the south terrace.

are executed with lawn rather than paving and palms rather than structure, used architecturally at the sides. Planting defines the larger themed gardens all around, so they flow together mostly without such intervening works as walls, fences, and gates.

The estate house has a door and a porte-cochere entry on the north side. The public entrance is at the east end through a loggia that the Huntingtons used as an outdoor room. Dense with large plants, the landscaping concentrates around these northeast-corner features. Standing out among trees are a spreading coast live oak (*Quercus agrifolia*) and three large *Brachychiton discolor* specimens in the circle. Rhapis palms, a tall white silk floss tree (*Chorisia insignis*) with a swollen green prickle-studded trunk, and a huge white-flowering *Talauma hodgsonii,* a relative of the magnolia from the Himalayas, surround the loggia. In the planting's lower story, bird of paradise (*Strelitzia reginae*) is prominent, but the stars of the show are cycads (see pp. 80–83). These primitive palmlike plants have grown into a thick screen in a rockery north of the loggia and are planted in several other locations. Here also are Australian tree fern and several other fern species. South of the loggia, a hundred-year-old English yew (*Taxus baccata* 'Elegantissima') forms a great green mass.

Lacebark trees (*Brachy-chiton discolor*) tower over an understory of Australian tree ferns and bird of paradise.

Running the length of the house, the broad south terrace has a balustrade topped by a line of ornamental urns. It also has clipped round pillars of Australian brush cherry (*Syzygium paniculatum*) that repeat the façade's architectural elements. Rearing south of the balustrade, two giant coral trees (*Erythrina caffra*) partly shade the terrace, as does a Moreton Bay chestnut (*Castanospermum australe*) at the south-east corner of the loggia.

West beyond the terrace in a protected corner of the house, a royal palm (*Roystonea*) of unidentified species from the Caribbean flourishes as yet unharmed by cold wind or frost. Other areas around the mansion—the rose garden on the west, and the Shakespeare garden and North Vista on the north—are discussed in the next few chapters.

Ferns and cycads thrive in this shady rockery next to the mansion's loggia. Hertrich intended the rockery for plants requiring semishade and protection against frosts. He found the porous rock, a soft tufa stone, near Santa Cruz, California. The Italian marble fountain is topped by a bronze statuette, *Bacchante* by Frederick MacMonnies (American, 1863–1937).

LEFT: The tufted heads of cycads (*Cycas revoluta*) and a majestic Moreton Bay chestnut (*Castanospermum australe*) flank a passage from the balustraded terrace to the broad lawns. The tree's orange and yellow flowers attract birds and butterflies in summer.

Intervals of green lawn serve as graceful transitions from one specialized, richly planted garden to another. This one separates the rose garden (displaying a profusion of the Floribunda rose 'Showbiz') and the varied skyline of the subtropical garden beyond.

OPPOSITE: On this sunny November day a few pink blossoms of early-flowering *Camellia japonica* can be seen at left. A cycad juts out just beyond the statue, inviting comparison with the similar-looking palms beyond.

· THE CYCAD COLLECTION ·
SURVIVORS FROM THE ERA OF DINOSAURS

ZOOLOGISTS CALL the Mesozoic Era the age of dinosaurs. Botanists call it the age of cycads, plant-world survivors known from the fossil record to have outlasted dinosaurs by 65 million years since those creatures met extinction. Cycads are the most primitive group of seed-producing plants, intermediate in evolutionary development between ferns and conifers, to which they are related. Like conifers, they do not produce flowers but bear their seed in cones. The Huntington collection has representatives of nine of the eleven cycad genera and half of the 150 or so known species. They appear in the landscaping of the Huntington Gallery and the Japanese garden as well as in the Australian, jungle, and desert gardens.

William Hertrich began the collection in 1910 with a few plants of *Ceratozamia mexicana* and *Dioon edule* that he brought back from Mexico. In 1913 he received a shipment of exceptional specimens, some reputed to be three to four hundred years old, from Japan. That same year he made a major purchase from collector Louis Bradbury of nearby Duarte. Later, the widow of Los Angeles oil baron Edward L. Doheny contributed a specimen of the exceedingly rare *D. merolae* to the Huntington collection.

Young cycads start out with the airy, lacy appearance of ferns and then eventually age into something resembling palms. Indeed, the most commonly grown cycad in Southern California, *Cycas revoluta*, is misleadingly called sago palm. The taller woody cycads grow very slowly, adding a new rosette of leaves at the top of a thick, columnar trunk each year, or none in cone-bearing years, so a plant might take more than a century to reach its ultimate height, which in some species can be dozens of feet tall. Pollen-producing male cones and seed-bearing female cones appear on separate plants, though not necessarily at the same time, so even with a male plant nearby a female may remain unpollinated.

Cycads are largely found in limited areas of Australia, Japan, Southeast Asia, South Africa, and tropical zones of the Americas. Some grow in shaded tropical

Cycads are palmlike in appearance and in name ("cycad" derives from the Greek "cyckos," which means palmlike) but are more closely related to conifers. What appear to be cycad flowers are actually cones, which often have intricate shapes.

forests, others grow in dry, open country where their leathery leaves are a response to arid conditions. Such genera as *Cycas* are widely distributed throughout Southeast Asia and northern Australia. More restricted in distribution are such others as *Encephalartos* and *Stangeria*, found only in South Africa, and *Bowenia*, *Lepidozamia*, and *Macrozamia*, found only in Australia.

    Their form and beauty have made cycads so popular as ornamentals and collector's items that to supply the market, many of them have become rare and endangered in their native habitats. In South Africa, for example, there may be more cycads in private gardens than are left in the wild. Some measures have been undertaken to protect natural populations. In South Africa, people are now required to have a permit to own cycads. In Australia, where for years ranchers destroyed macrozamias because of their toxicity to livestock, a Macrozamia National Park provides protection within its boundaries.

Cycad cones can sometimes resemble pineapples and weigh as much as eighty pounds. The smaller cones of *Encephalartos* (above) suggest pine cones. Male and female cones are produced on separate plants. *Cycas revoluta* (left and opposite page) has sago starch in its stems, giving the plant its common name of sago palm.

· THE NORTH VISTA ·
REINTERPRETING A FORMAL TRADITION

GRANDEST of the Huntington's gardens though little more than an acre in size, this grassy allée reaches from the Huntington Gallery north six hundred feet—the length of two football fields—to focus on an early baroque fountain backed by greenery and a spectacular wall of mountains. In a long European tradition of axial outdoor spaces related to buildings, it was the conception of Myron Hunt, architect of the Beaux Arts–style manor, who liked to design gardens for his estate houses. Nonetheless, this space was defined not by the structures expected in formal gardens of that time but by planting.

Several key elements establish the spirit of a garden from the baroque period, 1600 to 1750. One is the Italian stone fountain, complete with sculptured dolphins, that Henry Huntington bought knocked down in England and had shipped to San Marino for reassembly in a basin thirty-eight feet across. Another is a straight row of graceful fountain palms (*Livistona australis*) on either side of the seventy-five-foot-wide lawn. Arrayed architecturally against native oaks, their trunks form a living colonnade (with some gaps on the east side where a few of the original eleven palms are gone) that directs the eye toward the fountain. Sometime after palms were planted, eleven eighteenth-century Italian stone figures were placed on each side of

A colorful, informal planting of dome-shaped azaleas, backed by tall glossy camellias, in this case *Camellia japonica* 'Zambo', surrounds the garden statuary lining either side of the North Vista.

Stone dolphin detail on the baroque fountain

North Vista 1907

North Vista 1920

Native oaks dominated the site that was to become the North Vista (left). Years later palms surrounded by groomed hedges lined the allée (right) and a splendid baroque fountain (opposite) had been installed as the focal point at the north end.

the straight greensward, inward of the palms and repeating their rhythm. Later still, camellias filled in between palms and azaleas between statues, to create a flowering base for the colonnade. Two stone figure pairs, probably mid-eighteenth-century German, mark the grass rectangle's south end near the mansion, and disposed around an irregular lawn south of that are six other single figures and an Italian tempietto holding a nineteenth-century sculpture.

Through the oak woodland on three sides of the North Vista, pathways wind among plantings of camellias (see pp. 90–95), azaleas, and other shade-loving plants. Evergreen azaleas along the allée and the paths emphasize Southern Indicas. Near the north entrance to the east walkway are Satsuki azaleas, late-blooming plants that adapt well to bonsai culture. At the southeastern edge are several locally developed azalea cultivars that do well in Southern California. Begonias, fuchsias, gardenias, impatiens, spiraeas, violets, and several ferns are also part of the shaded understory.

· THE CAMELLIA COLLECTION ·
A PLANTSMAN'S LIFE WORK LIVES ON

The dark leaves and abundant soft pink peony-form flowers of *Camellia hiemalis* 'Showa Supreme' (opposite), all but obscure the fountain topped by a winged cherub. *C. hiemalis*, believed to be a hybrid between *C. sasanqua* and *C. japonica,* bloom longer and later than *C. sasanqua.* They are not found in the wild.

THE INTERNATIONAL CAMELLIA Society has named the Huntington as an International Camellia Garden of Excellence, one of five such gardens in the world. At the Huntington, camellias line roads and paths in some twelve acres in the central and western parts of the gardens. They are planted in native oak woodland on both sides of the North Vista and under mixed pine and oak on the slopes of North Canyon, north of the Japanese garden. With sixty species and twelve hundred cultivars of camellias, and others continually being added, this is one of the most comprehensive collections anywhere.

William Hertrich's lifelong work made the collection notable. Only one specimen remains from before he went to work for Henry Huntington in 1905, a splendid 'Pink Perfection' beside a path west of the North Vista, the oldest original camellia on the grounds. Hertrich began growing camellias from seed in 1912 as understock for grafting new varieties and for setting out along the North Vista and in North Canyon. Forty-two years later he published the results of his long-term opportunity to propagate, study, and photograph a thousand cultivars in his three-volume *Camellias in the Huntington Gardens.*

From his thirty-year effort Hertrich had many plants available for grafting by 1942, when the Southern California Camellia Society began to participate in the collection. After World War II the society agreed to donate plants and create a test garden, and the work of developing new cultivars began in earnest. Today the society organizes an annual camellia show at the Huntington.

Camellias originated in Asia and after a long history of cultivation the first

'Captain Rawes' was shown in *Curtis's Botanical Magazine* with its carmine rose red semi-double irregular petals. Compare this 1827 illustration with the photograph of the flower below.

Camellia japonica 'Henry E. Huntington' is a cultivar developed by Nuccio's Nurseries of Altadena, California, and released in 1995, the Huntington's seventy-fifth anniversary as an institution.

Camellia japonica reached the Western world in the early eighteenth century. Two camellias in the gardens represent the introduction of this species to England in 1792: *C. japonica* 'Alba Plena' and 'Variegata', both found along the upper walk in North Canyon. 'Alba Plena' is also found east of the North Vista. *C. japonica* has proven to be the most popular camellia species, with 50,000 named cultivars historically. It forms handsome shrubs or trees with broad, rounded, shiny foliage and single-to-double flowers that are seldom fragrant and range in color from white to red. Peak blooming season is January to March. One Huntington introduction is 'Margarete Hertrich' propagated by William Hertrich in 1944 and named after his wife. A medium white formal double with many small petals, it is still grown by camellia hobbyists. It grows along the central pathway in North Canyon. The Elegans variant cultivars of *C. japonica* give their name to Elegans Lane west of the North Vista.

Higo camellias, found mainly in the North Canyon, have a unique flower form. Much admired in Japan, where they are often used as bonsai plants, Higos are considered a style of flower rather than a species. They have been selected for centuries from *C. japonica* and probably the lesser-known *C. rusticana*, the snow camellia. With rare exceptions, the petals number between five and nine, may be uneven in length, and are often thick and leathery. Their most obvious features are the numerous stamens, with a count varying between 100 and 250. Sometimes matching the flower's coloring, they appear densely packed in a wide ring or crown, leaving the single pistil alone in the center.

A large selection of another species, *C. sasanqua*, introduced into England in 1811, is planted on the east hillside of North Canyon. Sasanquas bear profuse, small, often fragrant flowers in varied forms in white, pinks, and reds, from September into January. The plants have a more gracefully drooping, weeping, or spreading habit than japonicas. Two unusual ones are *C. sasanqua* 'Hugh Evans', with medium-pink single flowers, and 'Mine-no-Yuki', blanketed with peony-shaped flowers in early fall.

North Canyon and a knoll west of the North Vista fountain feature the first cultivars to be imported to North America of another important species, *C. reticulata*. Reticulatas are noted for huge pink, scarlet, mostly semi-double flowers, peaking March through

2784.

W.J.H.delt.   Pub.by S.Curtis.Walworth.Dec.1.1897.   Swan.Sc.

In the wild, camellia species have flowers composed of a single row of petals. Over the years so many forms of camellia flowers have been selected from the wild and through hybridization that flower forms are classified in six types based on the number and arrangement of the petals.

LEFT: *Camellia japonica* 'Pink Perfection' is a formal double type with petals that overlap.

TOP RIGHT: The deep rose pink 'John Anson Ford' is a semi-double, defined as having two or more rows of petals around a prominent stamen display.

BOTTOM RIGHT: 'Elena Nobile', a rose form of camellia, has layered petals that reveal the stamens in a concave center when fully opened.

May. Some specimens are the original plants imported in the mid-1940s from Kunming Botanical Garden in Yunnan Province, in mountainous south China, where reticulatas have been cultivated since 900 A.D.

A hybrid of *C. reticulata* first appeared in England in 1820 when Captain Richard Rawes, an East India merchantman, arrived with a number of camellia plants, among them a botanically unknown specimen from China. This 'Captain Rawes' cultivar (pictured on previous page) first flowered in 1826, creating a sensation with its very large semi-double rose pink flower. It can be seen along a path west of the North Vista. While reticulatas produce some of the most spectacular flowers in the genus, they grow as loosely branched, lanky shrubs or trees (up to fifty feet in height), less compact and attractive in habit than *C. japonica*.

Tea plants (*C. sinensis*), used to make green and black beverage teas, are located along the lower path in the North Canyon, so visitors can compare tea with the garden camellia. When taxonomists established the Tea family, Theaceae, they placed the tea plant as a related member of *Thea sinensis*. On further analysis, many taxonomists came to believe that the tea plant shared so many characteristics with

TOP LEFT: *Camellia reticulata* 'Otto Hopfer', a semi-double.

TOP RIGHT: 'Wilbur Foss', a full peony form with a domed mass of mixed irregular petals and petaloids.

BOTTOM LEFT: 'Berenice Boddy', a semi-double form, which is characterized by two rows of petals and conspicuous stamens.

BOTTOM RIGHT: *C. elegans* 'Splendor' is an anemone form, which usually has one or more rows of large outer petals lying flat or undulating and a convex mass of intermingled petaloids and stamens at its center.

other species in the genus *Camellia* that today it is grouped with the camellias.

Camellias growing near the waterfall in the canyon include *C. nitidissima*, a yellow camellia, and *C. lutchuensis*, the most fragrant species. *C. saluenensis*, important for developing new hybrids, is seen on the North Vista's east walk, and *C. granthamiana*, with large white flowers, at the southeast end of the North Vista. Species Lane, north of the hedge in the North Vista, has been planted with 50 species of camellias, some rare.

The Huntington has made some notable introductions. One is 'William Hertrich', a large, deep cherry red, semi-double seedling of a reticulata imported from China. Other introductions include 'Howard Asper', with salmon pink flowers; 'Flower Girl', with bright pink flowers; 'Beverly L. Baylies', a *C. saluenensis* hybrid with semi-double pink flowers that bloom early and profusely; 'Betty's Beauty', a sport of *C. japonica* 'Betty Sheffield'; 'Little Michael', a miniature, anemone flower type of *C. japonica;* and 'Carl Tourje', a hybrid of *C. pitardii* x *C. reticulata* with large, semi-double, wavy pink petals.

· THE SHAKESPEARE GARDEN ·
VIGNETTE OF AN ENGLISH COUNTRYSIDE

Purple hollyhocks and pink lilies

OPPOSITE: A sculptured bust of its patron poet presides over the Shakespeare garden and an audience of spring-blooming iris. Among the most successful bulblike plants for Southern California, iris do not require winter chilling and tolerate summer heat.

T HE SUMMER'S FLOWER is to the summer sweet," William Shakespeare wrote in Sonnet XCIV. He might have had in mind the spirit of this one-acre garden between the Huntington and Virginia Steele Scott art galleries. Here in the gardens' main showcase of annuals and flowering perennials a bust of the Bard of Avon contemplates some of the plants that figure in his own writings and in English gardens from the late sixteenth century to our time. In that tradition the flowers bloom most profusely through spring and summer.

This is the third version of a Shakespeare garden at the Huntington. Opened in 1959 as a living counterpart to Elizabethan literary works in the Library, the first was devoted only to plants specifically mentioned in Shakespeare. Since many of those failed in the decidedly non-English climate of the San Gabriel Valley, the garden was revised in 1972 to be more attractive year-round by adding other ornamental plants in use during the Elizabethan era in England and elsewhere.

In 1984 the setting changed with the construction of the Scott Gallery on the north, so the landscape was again redesigned, this time as a naturalistic English countryside setting to serve as a foreground to that building. Graded berms and a central dell or bog—dry except during the rainy season—with a bridge, lawn, and planting beds suggest a stylized pastoral glade against a backdrop of neighboring trees. On days of heavy visitation the paths efficiently move visitors between the galleries and from garden to garden, and this space functions as an unusually agreeable central plaza.

The classical façade of the Virginia Steele Scott Gallery is background for flowers from Shakespeare's time, including white oxeye daisies; pink blooms of crabapple at left.

OPPOSITE: Among the annuals and perennials mingling in this summer view are yellow yarrow; crimson lychnis, and pink and white common foxglove.

Small signs here and there in the beds supply Shakespeare quotations related to flowers, holly, and other plants. The garden is lush with perennials interwoven in an informal landscape with such flowers as buttercup, campanula, columbine, foxglove, geranium, goldenrod, iris, wormwood, and yarrow. Bulbs, lilies, and many iris make seasonal appearances. In the center, tall yellow spikes of verbascum (mullein) contrast with fountaining rushes and grasses and bold leaf forms. Near the south entrance, mounding feverfew (a chrysanthemum that bears small white flowers) reseeds among spreading rosemary.

Hedges and individual plants of holly, laurel, and viburnum provide masses of greenery, and flowering and fruiting trees—crabapple, lilac, pomegranate, and quince—flaunt spring color. Arbors with domes that echo the central dome of the Scott Gallery mark the east and south entrances and support grapevines and other climbing plants. An olive tree recalls Shakespeare's "olives of endless age" metaphor for peace and longevity in Sonnet CVII, proclaiming the writer will live on in his work.

THE ROSE GARDEN
A LIVING LIBRARY OF FLOWER HISTORY

The rose garden was originally planned as a spectacular massed display. Today the garden's forty beds have been planted with a living history of the rose. This pergola near the tea room supports climbers in shades of red, pink, and white. In the foreground is a bed filled with the yellow Floribunda rose 'Sun Flare'.

RIGHT: Named in honor of the seventy-fifth anniversary of the institution's founding, the 'Huntington's Hero' rose was propagated from a sport discovered on one of sixty bushes of 'Hero' in the rose garden's David Austin rose planting.

EST OF THE Huntington Gallery, the three-acre rose garden is one of the Huntington's themed areas that interpret plants in terms of culture and history—along with the Shakespeare, herb, and Japanese gardens. It is also one of the three gardens most popular with visitors, along with the Japanese and desert gardens. Its blooming peaks in April, with most roses flowering sometime from March through December. Pruning time is January; removing a third to half of the previous year's growth channels a plant's energy in the year ahead into flower production rather than growth.

While some kinds of plants in the botanical gardens have hardly changed in millions of years, few have altered more than roses, the most widely planted shrub and one of the most varied in breeding. In this garden, roses in beds and climbing on pergolas, arches, and a dome reveal a complex history that ranges over two and a half millennia from antiquity to the present. The garden displays nearly twelve hundred species and cultivars. They include examples from every important group in the rose's development and every Northern Hemisphere region where roses are native.

The garden was planned by Myron Hunt, architect of the estate house, as a formal space

'Altissimo', a Floribunda shrub rose that is grown most successfully as a climber

with an east-west axis meant to match that of the mansion's central hall. When the foundation was begun in 1909, however, Henry Huntington had the axis shifted a few degrees to preserve two old oaks (later taken out). William Hertrich had already planted the roses according to the original plan, so the two axial lines never coincided. Twice the size of the one today, that first rose garden was reduced in area in 1922. At that time many flower beds were replaced by lawn, and an eighteenth-century French stone tempietto with a sculpture was installed. Altered again several times over the years, the garden was last refurbished beginning in 1988. Meanwhile, after nine decades some of its specimen trees remain, grown now to monumental size. Among them are three Montezuma cypress (*Taxodium mucronatum*) from Mexico, a Queensland kauri (*Agathis robusta*), and several magnolias.

Today the garden contains forty beds planted to roses, including the climbing kinds. A walk through it reveals rose history from ancient to modern. Two pergolas shade a walk that runs along the north part of the garden from its northeast entrance to near the Japanese garden on the west. Plants in the bed south of the eastern pergola are from the first period of rose history, from as early as a fourth-century B.C. mention by Greek historian Herodotus to the end of the eighteenth century. Typically these old roses—Alba, Centifolia, Damask, Gallica, and Moss—bloom only in spring, in flat or cupped blossoms ranging in color from white, pink, and pale red through purple. Yellow was not unknown, but a true yellow did not appear until the twentieth century. One of the most celebrated old roses was Centifolia, the "hundred-leaved rose" noted in Latin literature. The Huntington's centifolias were developed by sixteenth- and seventeenth-century Dutch hybridizers.

Among these old roses are some mentioned by Shakespeare and in Renaissance herbals and rose books collected in the Library. Prominent in the display are the red rose of Lancaster (*Rosa gallica* 'Officinalis') and the white rose of York (*Rosa alba*). How they became emblems of opposing factions in the 1455–1485 Wars of the Roses is dramatized by Shakespeare in *King Henry VI, Part 1*. They are joined by the pink and white summer Damask rose 'York and Lancaster', symbol of reconciliation after the victorious Lancastrian Henry Tudor became king and married Elizabeth of York.

Two beds north of that pergola contain roses from the second major period of rose history, the nineteenth century, when China and Tea roses were introduced

In the mild climate of Southern California, roses flower from March through December, but the garden is in full bloom in mid-April. The porticoed entrance to the tea room is scarcely visible behind a cascade of climbing roses, including 'Cécile Brunner', along the length of the pergola. Some of the beds here are planted in the traditional cottage garden way, combining roses with herbs, annuals, and perennials. The roses in the foreground include the yellow Floribunda 'Mountbatten' and the dark pink Floribunda 'Matangi'.

into Europe from Asia. China roses are usually short plants with small to medium-sized flowers, often in clusters. An early one here is 'Slater's Crimson China', the first true bright red and parent of all modern red roses. Tea roses tend to be tall, with large flowers that often droop on weak stems. Though both are tender in cold climates, both share the important ability to bloom more than once in a season. It took workers from 1800 to the 1840s before the first hardy remontant, or repeat-flowering, roses were at last hybridized from China and Tea roses. In time some two thousand varieties resulted from that revolutionary feat, among them Bourbon, Noisette, Hybrid Perpetual Portland groups, and the first Hybrid Tea, 'La France'.

The third or modern period in rose history had its roots in three nineteenth-century advances: the appearance of the Hybrid Tea and Polyantha varieties and of a true yellow rose color. Introduced in 1867, Hybrid teas, considered to be backcrosses between Hybrid Perpetual and Tea roses, were destined to become the twentieth century's most popular roses, with thousands of varieties known. Introduced in France around 1870, Polyanthas were hybrids of *Rosa multiflora* by a China rose and became popular as short, compact plants with large clusters of small flowers. In 1910, a French cultivar, 'Soleil d'Or', crossed with Hybrid teas, became the parent of all modern yellow and bicolor roses.

Most of the garden's beds are devoted to Hybrid Tea, Polyantha, Floribunda, Grandiflora, Miniature, and other modern roses. Floribundas, pioneered in Denmark in the 1930s, are descendants of the Polyanthas with small stature and cluster bloom, used here massed as low borders to front taller varieties. Grandifloras are a cross of Hybrid Tea with Floribunda.

LEFT TO RIGHT: The climbing Floribunda 'Winifred Coulter Climbing' threads through one of the specially designed metal arches. A sport of the shrub rose 'Winifred Coulter', it flowers continuously and grows as high as fifteen feet. 'Cherry Vanilla Grandiflora' is pink with a golden heart. The apricot-colored 'Norwich Castle' is a relative newcomer, raised in 1979 by Peter Beales in Britain.

OPPOSITE: Lush pink Polyantha is weeping 'China Doll.'

Beds on both sides of the walk south from the center, at the restaurant entrance between pergolas, and west of the tempietto contain Floribunda and Hybrid Tea or Floribunda alone. West of that walk are eight beds of Hybrid Teas, Floribundas, and Grandifloras introduced since 1950.

East of the walk are two beds planted to very different roses. One of these contains roses from the California gold country planted during and after the 1849 Gold Rush and overlooked until our time, when Clair Martin, curator of the rose collection, found them growing in old gardens, cemeteries, and other locations. Most are no longer known commercially, but have been identified from early rose books and catalogs in the Library. The other contains English roses, a class of large shrubs developed since 1961 by English hybridizer David Austin. He combined the form, fragrance, and growth habit of once-blooming old roses with the repeat-blooming trait and color range of modern roses.

Along the central walk running west of the temple are planted climbers, All-American Rose Selections, and new introductions. South of that walk are a bed each of Hybrid Tea and Polyantha from 1867 to the 1910s and from the 1920s, a bed of Hybrid Tea, Floribunda, and Polyantha from the 1930s and two beds from the 1940s.

Along and near the west walk are beds of such specialty varieties as 'Peace', 'Ophelia', and 'Koster' roses and their sports on one side and plantings of wild roses and close hybrids from among more than two hundred known species on the other side.

'Altissimo' grows up the wall next to the tearoom entrance.

BELOW: Mid-April in the rose garden: in the foreground Hybrid Tea roses are carefully graded according to height; the Hybrid Tea 'Snowbird' climbs up the arch in the background.

Violet trumpet vine (*Clytostoma callistegioides*) drapes itself behind a fine display of 'Givenchy', a richly scented Hybrid Tea rose named for the perfume maker.

· THE HERB GARDEN ·
PLANTS FOR TASTE, SCENT, HEALTH, COLOR

Nebraska paving bricks separate beds of herbs grouped by uses, including the tussie mussie (nosegay) bed in middle of picture. Red dianthus bloom in foreground.

RIGHT: The autumn-flowering saffron crocus (*Crocus sativus*) is the source of the expensive spice saffron. The long red stigmas, twining through orange anthers, are cut, dried, and ground into a powder used for coloring and flavoring.

A HALF-ACRE FORMAL GARDEN planted to hundreds of kinds of herbs is tucked in a corner north of the rose garden and west of a patio restaurant remodeled from the estate's former billiard room and bowling alley. Installed in the 1950s, the garden reopened in its present form in 1976. Around an eighteenth-century German wrought-iron wellhead as a centerpiece, its separate beds group plants by use: culinary, salad herbs, teas, liqueur, medicinal, perfume and cosmetic, dye, potpourri and sachet, and nosegays. Other beds hold such specialties as rosemaries, rugosa and sweetbrier roses, and lavender. Some herbs are perennials but many are annuals, flowering bulbs, or deciduous perennials that die back after their growing seasons, so much of the planting is changed seasonally.

Not a botanical but a colloquial term, "herb" has many definitions, none of them precise. Cooks often restrict the meaning to leaves of low-growing annuals, perennials, and shrubs, but this garden takes a broader view: An herb is a plant whose parts—leaves, flowers, seeds, roots, and bark—have such special traditional uses as those noted above.

Like the Shakespeare garden, this one has living references to plant material recorded in the Library's collection of rare sixteenth- and seventeenth-century herbals. Those books contain botanical data, recipes, remedies,

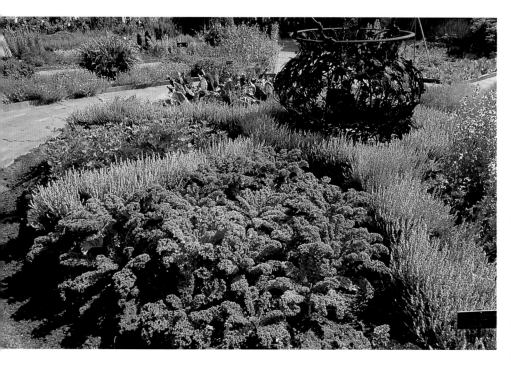

and other information about diet, health, and economic concerns in periods from medieval Europe to the settlement of North America. They describe many herbs that are obscure today and others familiar over the centuries.

The most widely known are those of American and European kitchen gardens, the likes of basil, bay laurel, marjoram, oregano, rosemary, sage, savory, tarragon, and thyme. Others are seasonings from other lands, increasingly enlarging the American food repertoire, such as Mexican oreganos, Southeast Asian lemongrass, and Vietnamese cilantro. A salad-herb

The bed around the wrought iron wellhead is sectioned off with a border of cat thyme and is changed seasonally. Curly leaf kale, foreground, is featured in spring and summer.

bed grows bronze fennel, nasturtium, parsley, and radicchio, while red-leaf basil in summer alternates with red-leaf lettuce in winter. A bed of confectionery herbs has horehound, a non-native widely naturalized in California; rose geranium, violets, and others. Two beds hold herbs that flavor wines and liqueurs and those whose leaves and other parts make teas and similar infusion drinks.

A bed of curative plants contains *Aloe vera,* an ancient specific for burns and other skin healing, as well as foxglove, larkspur, and *Catharanthus roseus,* from which chemicals used in treating leukemia can be extracted.

Plants were the main source for dyes until anilines and other chemicals came into use in the nineteenth century. A highly prized red came from madder (*Rubia tinctoria*). Leaves of woad (*Isatis tinctoria*) produced a blue that ancient Britons used not only for fabrics but to color their skin to intimidate even such sophisticated attackers as the invading Romans. Shades of yellow came from coreopsis, mullein, several marigolds, and calendulas.

Four beds hold such cosmetic herbs as jojoba, used in shampoos, and such fragrance sources as gardenia, rose, and violet. One grows lavenders, roses, lemon verbena, and others used in potpourri and for petal-strewing on festive occasions. The charming idea of flowers as herbs appears in a tussie mussie, or nosegay, bed of blossom symbolisms. The floral code is an ancient tradition. In *Hamlet*, Shakespeare's audiences knew exactly what the fair Ophelia meant when she declaimed of pansies for thoughts, fennel and columbine for strength and folly, daisy and violet for innocence and modesty, and "There's rosemary, that's for remembrance."

The lavender-purple flow-
ers of *Iris pallida* grace the
herbaceous borders; the
rhizomes are of value too
in perfume and potpourri.

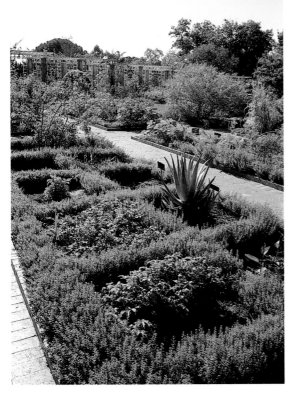

LEFT: Rectangular plant-
ing beds edged with bush
germander (*Teucrium
fruticans*) enclose plants
from which medicinals
can be extracted: foxglove
(*Digitalis purpurea*) for the
heart; feverfew (*Tanacetum
parthenium*) for headaches;
and *Aloe vera* for burns.

· THE JAPANESE GARDEN ·
ELEVEN CENTURIES OF TRADITION

A nineteenth-century Japanese house crowns the west side of the canyon in the Japanese garden. The swordlike foliage of the cycads at left guards the entrance to the moon bridge, visible at right.

TWO STONE LION-DOGS guard a gate west of the rose garden beyond which the visitor descends into a nine-acre canyon garden. The understated entry gives little hint of the visual surprise to come: a descendant of a traditional Japanese garden, as interpreted in twentieth-century America.

With none of the broad spaces and geometry of European garden tradition, this is an informal space to stroll through. Like a good suspense novel, it tantalizes the stroller's curiosity to see what lies ahead while changing views and small landscape events slow his progress and divert his attention: an exquisitely pruned pine, a stone lantern, a miniature pagoda, a tiny shrine. The garden alternates open with intimate passages, structures and accessories with skillfully manipulated planting. Using sophisticated artifice to achieve simplicity and identification with nature, it projects a sense of tranquility.

Begun in 1911, the Huntington's Japanese garden is one of America's oldest, most elaborate, and most gracefully matured. It has three parts. The main section is laid out as a stroll garden with a traditional house. A second section, added in 1968, is a walled compound containing a *karesansui* (dry landscape garden) and bonsai court. A third, added in 1970, is an informal three-acre garden

A tile-capped, earth-colored wall surrounds an expanse of raked gravel meant to evoke the feeling of a body of water interrupted here and there by rocks, symbolizing islands, and backed by trees and shrubs that suggest the far shore. The garden is similar to one in the main abbot's quarters in the celebrated Daitokuji temple in Kyoto.

OPPOSITE: Fall color comes when fallen ginkgo leaves blanket the dwarf mondo grass planted as ground cover. The plain stucco wall dramatizes both the forms and shadows of the trees.

of Asian plants, among them groves of golden and black bamboo. In 1973 an Ikebana house was erected outside the public area, where members of the San Marino League, a garden support group, study the art of ikebana, a Japanese style of flower arranging, and create displays for use in the Japanese house.

Why an Oriental garden here amid so much Occidental tradition? Things Japanese were of widespread fascination in 1911, scarcely sixty years since Commodore Matthew Calbraith Perry opened the reclusive island empire to the outside world. In the next few decades, America marveled at Japanese gardens in expositions at Philadelphia, Chicago, San Francisco, and St. Louis. Accounts by travelers to Japan, among them Edward S. Morse's 1885 *Japanese Homes and Their Surroundings*, stirred the national imagination. In the early twentieth century that book influenced architects Greene and Greene of Pasadena, among others, to a whole new aesthetic of structure related to landscape. By then Japanese gardens had become the height of fashion for those who could afford them. Some were small tea-ceremony gardens, but in Los Angeles two of estate size were built in the Hollywood Hills in 1912, one of them by Myron Hunt, Huntington's own architect. Meanwhile, George T. Marsh, proprietor of the famous Japanese garden for the 1894 San Francisco exposition, had opened a commercial tea garden in Pasadena.

Thus there were ample information and even design guidelines available when

Ornamental fruit trees lend seasonal color to the Japanese garden. In North Canyon the white-blossomed peach, *Prunus persica*, flowers early, a welcome harbinger of spring.

Huntington and Hertrich decided on an Oriental garden. Among them was Josiah Conder's *Landscape Gardening in Japan*, published in 1893, a copy of which Hertrich owned. The chosen site was a former reservoir, overgrown with brush, on the west side of San Marino Ranch. Fortuitously, when Hertrich approached Marsh seeking to buy Oriental plants, he found the tea garden failing financially, so though the plants were not for sale the whole might be. Huntington, accustomed to buying entire libraries and collections, snapped up the ensemble. Then came a mighty effort at earth moving, dismantling Marsh's Japanese house, boxing plants and ornaments, planting, and reassembling the house—all in record time, as Hertrich described it. There was some urgency, for Huntington wanted the garden completed by the end of 1912, when his new residence was to be occupied. That likely anticipated his impending second marriage, in 1913, and he may have intended the garden as a present for his new bride, Arabella.

Hertrich designed the garden and supervised its creation. He hired a Japanese craftsman to build its centerpiece arch bridge and a tile-roofed pavilion for a bronze temple gong. He also imported more garden accessories from Japan and over the years added other plantings. By World War II the house and garden had fallen into disrepair, but in the 1950s they were refurbished, largely through the San Marino League's efforts, and opened in 1958.

Junipers drape over a cement arch bridge, creating a reflection in the pond.

Inside the garden gate, a wisteria-shaded path leads down to a terrace and a first stunning view over the main garden and across to the house. An arch bridge and a smaller flat one span the pond. Beside it are a golden Niobe willow, a dense cluster of cycads (*Cycas revoluta*), and an evolving display of junipers and pines pruned and shaped for form. Pathways cross a lawn, climb the canyon sides, and follow a watercourse upstream.

Part of Japanese garden mystique is that the color green should be dominant, to induce a restful effect with none of the bright hues of, say, English flower gardens. That happens here, though a surprising amount of color plays a lesser, largely seasonal role. Much of it comes in spring from wisterias on arbors. The pond has colorful water lilies, lotus, and koi darting and flashing when sunlight catches their brilliant color. Mounding azaleas burst into bloom in late winter and spring on the slopes below the house. Flowering plum, cherry, and peach trees blossom from January through April. Sweet olive (*Osmanthus fragrans*) trees near the house add a pervasive sweet fragrance with their tiny white flowers. Several varieties of Japanese maple (*Acer palmatum*) sport red leaves in spring and summer and yellow in the fall—when the maidenhair trees (*Ginkgo biloba*) turn a bright yellow.

Pines, especially those native to Japan, are important features of Japanese gardens. Handsomely groomed Japanese red pines (*Pinus densiflora*), including

ABOVE: The curving trunk of a mature oak and a young maple create the impression of an arch framing the pagoda. Winding paths in this stroll garden alternately reveal and conceal views.

LEFT: The winter sun highlights the glossy green heads of *Cycas revoluta* and blossoms of the flowering peach *(Prunus persica* 'Icicle') by the arch bridge.

the 'Pendula' cultivar, are prominent around the stroll garden in single and multiple-trunked, weeping, and other forms. Many Japanese black pines (*P. thunbergii*), pruned and shaped as meticulously as bonsai, stand out on an island in the pond by a stone Buddha, on central garden slopes, and on slopes around the walled compound.

The canyon's west side is topped by a five-room nineteenth-century house from Japan. The Japanese orient the interiors of their houses to gardens outside. This one shows how traditional features accomplish that goal: the *engawa*, a veranda or floor-level platform that affords room-to-room

Japanese maples (*Acer palmatum*), among the most decorative of foliage trees, bring a touch of amber to the garden in the fall and a rich crimson in spring when new leaves appear.

passage outside; shoji, sliding exterior panels covered in translucent mulberry paper that close off rooms or open them to the garden; and *amado*, outer sliding shutters that close the house at night or during rain. Its interior features include *fusuma,* sliding wall panels that open up or close off rooms; *tokonoma*, alcoves for the reverential display of a flower arrangement, scroll, and other objects; and tatami, rush-covered straw floor mats in modular sizes that determine the size and shape of rooms. Though this is not a tea house, the utensils necessary for the tea ceremony are found in the north room. One of the most important rituals in Japanese culture, the tea ceremony is a traditional gathering of a host and several guests.

South of the house is a display of bonsai and suiseki, water-worn rocks in the shape of miniature landscapes. Beyond, steps lead down to a zigzag bridge across a dry landscape of stones. The idea that the purpose of a zigzag bridge is to thwart pursuit by evil spirits, known to travel only in straight lines, may be apocryphal, but the form is also a practical way to span a stream.

Then steps ascend a slope planted to mock orange (*Pittosporum tobira*) pruned to resemble billowy clouds, and then to a rectangular garden inside a tile-capped wall.

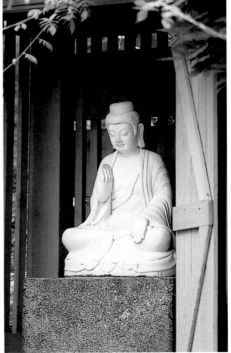

A small shrine to Buddha reflects the serenity of the garden.

This zigzag bridge crosses a dry streambed, where stones evoke the presence of rushing water. Clipped shrubs on either side of the steps are the Japanese *Pittosporum tobira.*

ABOVE: The bonsai court features examples of trees pruned on a miniature scale in shallow pots. On the ground in front is an example of *suiseki*, natural stones that suggest in miniature such landforms as a distant mountain or an island in the sea.

RIGHT: Tatami, mats made of compressed rice straw with a woven rush surface, cover the raised floor in the Japanese house.

OPPOSITE: A snow lantern looks out over a stand of green and yellow variegated dwarf bamboo and a magnificent Japanese red umbrella pine.

Here on one side of a central slate walk an expansive dry garden of raked gravel, a few stones, and background shrubbery make a stylized, abstract reference to islands in a sea, a scene whose interpretation depends upon the viewer's own imagination. On the other side, ginkgos over a ground cover of dwarf mondo grass (*Ophiopogon japonicus* 'Nana') similarly evoke a forest. Past a far gate, a small court displays bonsai, those often old dwarfed trees in shallow containers kept shaped by continual pruning of leaves, branches, and roots. At one end of the court a path leads down through a shady forest of giant bamboo and tall trees, mostly from Asia, to the garden's lower exit.

PAGES 124–125: The subtropical garden displays such beauties as the Brazilian coral tree *Erythrina falcata*.

In The Gardens, Part III:

The Newer Gardens

· THE AUSTRALIAN GARDEN ·
TREES THAT CHANGED THE FACE OF CALIFORNIA

Eucalyptus dominate in height and in number in the Australian garden. The oldest specimens, like the tall and elegant *Eucalyptus citriodora* at left, were planted in the 1940s. The Huntington has nearly one-fourth of the 700 known eucalyptus species, showing their remarkable range of height and growth habit, leaf form and color, bark texture and color, often long-lasting flowers, and sculptural fruits and pods.

RIGHT: Gardeners appreciate the fernlike leaves and amber-colored spring and summer flowers of the fast-growing silky oak (*Grevillea robusta*), and furniture makers prize its wood.

THE RECTANGULAR AUSTRALIAN garden covers five acres of level terrace ground directly below and parallel to the subtropical garden. Stretching from the lily pond area to the Japanese garden, this naturalistic, partly parklike passage of trees and shrubs mostly native to Australia is dominated by eucalyptus. A tramp through its meadows and groves makes a pleasant contrast to a walk on paths through the more manicured gardens on the hilltop above.

Like palms, eucalyptus early on became a California tradition. Palms may be the Southern California symbol, but no trees more drastically altered the face of the state than eucalyptus, the most widely planted of all imports. Eucalyptus enthusiasm began in the nineteenth century and peaked in a craze of planting for timber and railroad ties even as Henry Huntington was developing his gardens. Less interested in mass than in selective planting, he put in only a few, among them lemon-scented gums (*Eucalyptus citriodora*) near today's patio restaurant and next to his mausoleum.

Widespread interest continued, and in 1928, after Huntington's death, William Hertrich had some rare and interesting eucalyptus installed in a northeast part

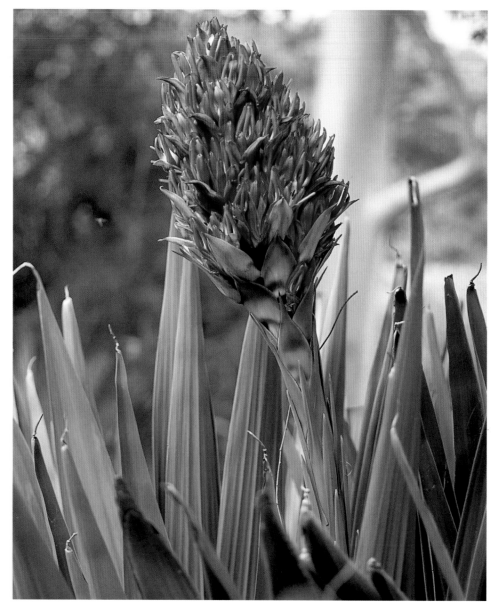

The giant spear lily, *Doryanthes palmeri,* may grow as tall as eight feet.

OPPOSITE: *Eucalyptus deglupta*, from the Philippines, is prized for its multicolored bark and leaves that are aromatic when crushed.

of the property now devoted to visitor parking. In 1943 a thousand trees supplied by the U.S. Department of Agriculture were planted in close rows on the site of a former orange grove south of the estate house. Later all but fifty were taken out. Those veterans form the nucleus of today's Australian garden, opened to the public in 1964 after many other plants had been added.

Eucalyptus is one of the largest genera in Australia, with some 700 species. The garden has more than 100 species, both trees and shrubs. Placed among them are acacias, callistemons, cassias, grevilleas, melaleucas, and others from the island continent's semiarid regions. At the garden's southeastern end a collection of New Zealand natives includes coprosmas, phormiums and other plants notable as landscape subjects more for leaf and structure than for flowers.

Mottlecah (*Eucalyptus macrocarpa*) has the largest flowers and fruits of all eucalyptus. As the red stamens appear, the hard white bud cap (top), actually the fused petals, falls off. Fluffy red stamens push apart the gray-green leaves ranged along sprawling horizontal branches (opposite bottom).

Many trees have grown to monumental height, among them the tall, straight, fast-growing Sydney blue gum (*E. saligna*). A young mountain ash (*E. regnans*), the tallest eucalyptus and tallest of all hardwood (flowering) trees, grows in the southeast part of the garden. Set out among the trees, many other smaller, shrubby eucalyptus called mallees are famous for showy flowers of yellow, pink, and red.

Here too are acacias, of which Australia also has hundreds of species. In the garden they stand out for their winter and spring bloom with masses of tiny yellow blossoms and silvery foliage. Specimens of silky oak (*Grevillea robusta*), with orange-yellow flowers in late spring, rival some of the old eucalyptus trees in size, height, and girth. Brachychitons are seen here as large specimens alone and in groves that include *B. rupestris* with its distinctive bottle-shaped trunk. Melaleucas are represented by the chenille honey-myrtle (*M. huegelii*), with spikes of white flowers in late spring, from western Australia; and the scarlet honey-myrtle (*M. fulgens*). A young gum myrtle (*Angophora costata*) will grow to a tall tree that resembles eucalyptus in size, habit, and foliage.

The large trees are seen from the road along the south side or a path along the north, while a walk through the interior reveals more variety. Plants of one of Australia's four cycad genera, *Macrozamia,* are seen in the garden. The spear lily (*Doryanthes palmeri*) and gymea lily (*D. excelsa*) are spectacular in spring with six-foot or longer flower stalks and large red flowers above tall sword-leaf clumps. Two plants have copious lavender flowers, the fragrant-leaved mint bush (*Prostanthera rotundifolia*), and blue hibiscus (*Alyogyne huegelii*). Standing out among fifteen species of cassias are feathery cassia (*Cassia artemisioides*) and silver cassia (*C. phyllodinea*); both have bright yellow flowers and silvery, feathery leaves. The oddest plants of all are the kangaroo paws (*Anigozanthos* spp.), with truly bizarre, fuzzy yellow, red, or green flowers atop thin red stalks.

Melaleuca halmaturorum is one of the many melaleucas called paperbark after their spongy, papery bark.

Anigozanthos flavidus is known as the kangaroo paw because of the clawlike shape of its tubular flowers. Carried on stems up to six feet tall, these are usually greenish yellow, sometimes yellow, orange, or red. Although many species bloom in winter, this one is summer-flowering.

· THE SUBTROPICAL GARDEN ·
PLANTS FROM MEDITERRANEAN CLIMATES

Stunning *Tabebuia impetiginosa* displays its fuchsia-colored trumpet-shaped blooms from late winter to early spring

I N THIS four-acre garden, "subtropical" refers to plants that can survive a light frost but are likely to perish when the temperature drops well below freezing. Occupying the estate's warmest spot and best protected from cold, the garden tests plants whose long-term performance in the San Gabriel Valley climate remains to be learned. On the slope below the Huntington Gallery and rose garden and above the Australian garden, it extends east from the Japanese garden to the jungle garden.

The garden displays bulbs, shrubs, trees, and other non-succulent plants from subtropical regions. With such diversity it lacks the orderly appearance of the more structured gardens and its unfamiliar species make it of special interest to botanists and other plant enthusiasts. Represented are the Mediterranean region and areas of similar climate in South Africa, Chile, and islands in the eastern North

RIGHT: The long seedpods of the golden trumpet tree (*Tabebuia chrysotricha*) split open when mature to release winged seeds.

Atlantic—particularly the Canaries—as well as warm-temperate and subtropical Africa, Southeast Asia, and the Americas. Not represented are Mediterranean-climate parts of Australia, which have their own adjacent garden, or California, seen in other Southern California botanical gardens devoted to native plants.

Many plants here came from Huntington staff expeditions to Mexico, others were sent by plant explorers from around the world, and some by exchange with other botanical gardens. The planting arrangement has been informal, loosely arranged by geographic origin: Mexico in the center and toward the eastern end, southern Africa in the west and center, Mediterranean in the northwest, and southeast Asia and the Americas to the east.

Along the several paths lacing the slope the most prominent—and permanent—features are flowering trees. Cassias put forth yellow flowers in late summer and fall. Winter brings out bloom on coral trees of several species, one of them a spectacular hybrid, *Erythrina* x *sykesii*.

Golden trumpet tree (*Tabebuia chrysotricha*) blooms on bare branches in early spring, then leaves appear. *Wigandia urens*, with deep purple spring flowers and huge leaves, stands out like a beacon. The more shrublike tree dahlia (*Dahlia imperialis* 'Plena') has pinkish purple flowers. Late spring and on into summer bring the blue flowers of the jacarandas and pink flowers on the landmark cape chestnut (*Calodendrum capense*).

This garden has more color on the ground than most. It comes from dozens of South African bulbs in bloom at different times of the year and such ground covers as *Gazania uniflora* and *Arctotheca calendula* (cape weed), a vigorous yellow daisy.

Among several Huntington introductions are the Acapulco daisy (*Zinnia maritima*), a ground cover; the 'Irving Cantor' agapanthus, with low foliage and blue flowers on three-foot stalks; and *Salvia* 'Purple Majesty', part of a remarkable salvia collection.

A little off the paths grow the rare *Deppea splendens*, extinct in the wild, and such curiosities as the canary bird bush (*Crotalaria agatiflora*) and *Boehmeria nivea*, from which ramie fiber is extracted.

Opposite: A spectacular burst of color occurs in October and November with the flowering of *Gladiolus dalenii*, from which our modern hybrids derive.

Above: Pink powder puff (*Calliandra haematocephala*) is a winter-blooming evergreen or semideciduous shrub.

Bottom right: The marmalade bush (*Streptosolen jamesonii*), an evergreen shrub that can reach eleven feet, displays its orange-red flowers in the subtropical garden.

Bottom left: Chameleon-like flowers of the shrubby vine *Combretum fruticosum* turn from chartreuse to yellow to orange-red.

· THE JUNGLE GARDEN ·
TROPICAL FANTASY FOR A SUBTROPICAL CLIMATE

A fretwork of leaves dapples the cooling waterfall at the heart of the four-acre jungle garden. The *Ficus auriculata* on the right was already here, part of a forest of ornamental fig trees, when this garden was opened in 1979. On the left, Australian tree fern (*Cyathea cooperi*) with its lacy foliage relishes the damp atmosphere, and Abyssinian banana (*Ensete ventricosum*) raises high its tattered leaves in the background.

RIGHT: Hibiscus flowers are solitary beauties, their paper-thin petals a marvel of subtle shading and a reminder of the tropics.

RATHER THAN TRY to reproduce an equatorial rain forest, this four-acre garden creates tropical ambience with species that thrive in a subtropical climate. Suggesting the riotous growth of the hot and humid low latitudes, this multilayered environment has a high forest canopy, understory trees and shrubs, vines climbing tree trunks, leaves of often gargantuan proportions, but especially plants that people associate with the tropics. Grand old evergreen fig trees (*Ficus thonningii*) spread shade over bamboos, bananas, bromeliads, cycads, ferns, gingers, palms, and philodendrons. A waterfall and a stream tumbling down through this cool, dim retreat encourage moisture-loving plants. Located on a south-facing hillside with the same warm microclimate that benefits the adjacent subtropical garden, this informal, wild landscape also merges with the palm garden, visually borrowing its tropical effect.

The stream, completed in 1978, fills the lily ponds below. Near the ponds rears the most remarkable tree in the jungle garden if not on the entire estate, an ombú (*Phytolacca dioica*). Fast-growing, tall (to sixty feet) and nearly as wide, native to the plains of Argentina, it is that nation's unofficial emblem. A gnarled old specimen grown from seed received from the Buenos Aires Botanical Garden in 1912, this ombú has an enormous swollen base,

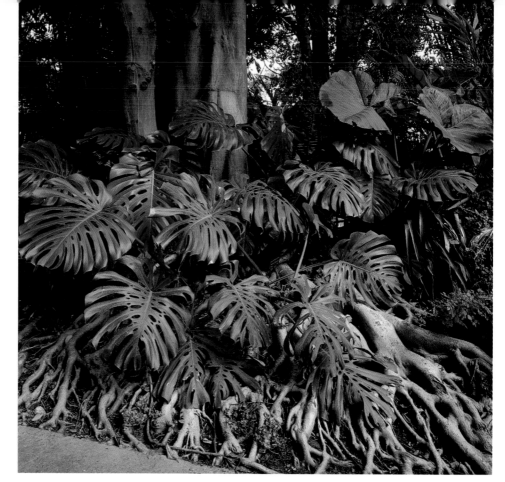

Massive leaves of the elephant ear plant (*Xanthosoma*) and split-leaf philodendron (*Monstera deliciosa*) clothe the intricate root system of an ornamental fig tree. The edible fruits of *Monstera* taste of pineapple and banana.

OPPOSITE: A walk, wild in feeling, from the waterfall to the Huntington Gallery is lined with *Pritchardia* palms and old specimens of the cycad *Encephalartos ferox*. In spring and late summer (first half of September) the small red flowers of *Billbergia* 'Huntington' appear. Later in the year the nectar-producing flowers of bird of paradise (*Strelitzia reginae*) and the luminous red flowers of the coral tree brighten the walk.

part of an above-ground root system that evolved for water storage as an adaptation to grass fires, winds, and scarce rainfall of the pampas.

The jungle garden's bananas and their relatives, the heliconias and strelitzias, rank high for tropical image. Among banana species grown as ornamentals is *Musa ornata,* with showy pink bracts. A relative of the banana, traveler's tree (*Ravenala madagascariensis*) may derive its name from a tendency to orient itself under natural conditions on a north-south axis, supposedly acting as a compass to travelers.

The garden has two of the few New World bamboos in cultivation, Mexican weeping bamboo (*Otatea acuminata*) up near the waterfall, and *Chusquea coronalis*, near the eastern edge. Another bamboo, the rare *Dendrocalamus asper,* also grows near the waterfall.

To take advantage of the warm microclimate, tropical palms are planted on both sides of the boundary with the palm garden next door. Seen along the paved walk are *Chamaedorea elatior*, a rare climbing palm, *Pritchardia* spp., native to Hawaii and other Pacific islands, and fishtail palm (*Caryota urens*). Cycads also contribute lacy, palmlike foliage, as do Australian tree ferns (*Cyathea cooperi*), with distinctive silver-dollar leaf scars on the trunk.

Ginger family genera *Hedychium* and *Alpinia* contribute bright colors in the dark forest, and split-leaf philodendron (*Monstera deliciosa*) and other plants add bold leaf forms. So do *Philodendron* 'Evansii', an arborescent or treelike plant, and

Strong forms of the conifer collection loom beyond the edge of the jungle garden. Lining the sloping path are clumps of mondo grass (*Ophiopogon japonicus*), pierced by the striking yellow-green and pink-green foliage of anthuriums and bromeliads.

OPPOSITE: The lower side of the garden, close to the lily ponds, enjoys a warm, sheltered microclimate. Here is the strawberry snowball tree (*Dombeya cacuminum*), a native of Madagascar, whose lovely scented flowers are sometimes hidden by luxuriant leaves.

a great-leaved elephant ear (*Xanthosoma*), near the waterfall. Philodendrons also grow in trees, though not as parasites, and some survive there as epiphytes after their connecting stem dies away. Other epiphytes that cling to trees include ferns, bromeliads, and the cacti *Rhipsalis* and *Epiphyllum*. Among lianas, large woody vines that hang from trees, is *Aristolochia brasiliensis* from Brazil. Forest-floor plants include such terrestrial bromeliads as pineapple (*Ananas bracteatus*) and species of *Pitcairnia*. Bromeliads that are naturally epiphytes are also used as ground covers here: *Aechmea, Billbergia, Nidularium, and Neoregelia*.

Many bromeliads are stemless perennials with colorful bracts and showy flowers that often last for months. A sampling of the species in the jungle garden is pictured here.

<small>OPPOSITE PAGE</small>

<small>LEFT:</small> The brightly colored bracts of *Portea petropolitana* compose its long-lasting four-foot flower stalks, which project from stiff swordlike leaves.

<small>TOP RIGHT:</small> Easy to grow, *Billbergia pyramidalis* takes its name from its pyramid-shaped flower spike.

<small>BOTTOM RIGHT:</small> The flowers of *Hohenbergia stellata* last for months. Its name refers to the starlike form of the compact spikes of the flowers.

<small>THIS PAGE</small>

<small>TOP LEFT:</small> The rose-colored torch of *Quesnelia arvensis* is studded with tiny dark blue and white flowers.

<small>TOP RIGHT:</small> *Aechmea fasciata* is the most popular and widely planted bromeliad in the world. Its rosy pink flower bracts have pale blue flowers that change to deep rose.

<small>BOTTOM:</small> The inflorescence of this *Aechmea ornata* is attractive even though it is almost through blooming —a few light pink flowers are still visible on top.

· THE HELEN AND PETER BING ·
CHILDREN'S GARDEN
PLAYFUL KINETIC SCULPTURES ARE SCIENCE IN DISGUISE

Is it a llama? A camel? This stately topiary creature stands guard over a corner of the children's garden.

BELOW: Sculpted black ravens stalk an oversize apple on a slab bench

CHILDREN OF ALL AGES have been climbing, crawling, touching, and exhaustively exploring the unusual features of the children's garden since it opened in 2004.

One feature, the Rainbow Room, sounds like it might be a cocktail lounge in a tropical island hotel, but rather it is one of the garden's nine kinetic "sculptures." To experience this feature, youngsters walk through mist released every fifteen minutes from overhead sprinklers and see a rainbow, even when it's not raining. In fact, it only works on sunny days!

All of the hands-on sculptures demonstrate a scientific principle related to earth, fire, air, or water, the themes of the garden, providing young children (primarily ages two to seven) with a variety of sensory experiences. In addition to visiting the Rainbow Room, youngsters can disappear into a sea of billowing fog, hold the kinetic energy of magnetic sand, and see and feel the effects of sound waves moving through water in a sonic pool. To view a colorful prism of light, little people crawl through a tunnel under a hill hidden by plants; in the center, shafts of refracted light appear in the darkened chamber.

The fire exhibit is a topiary volcano, a conical structure covered with jasmine, which can be experienced in-

Above left: Open-air garden house has child-size furniture inside.

Above right: Jasmine covers lower part of the volcano structure, New Zealand flax spews out the top.

side or out. At the peak, fog jets emit steam periodically, and colorful New Zealand flax in the center looks like an erupting volcano.

Playful plant choices, like topiary animals, weeping mulberry trees, papyrus, and tree aloes that resemble Dr. Seuss creations, generate a storybook atmosphere that combines elements of fantasy with the wonder of nature.

Parents and grandparents are not forgotten here. They can watch their children from umbrella-shaded benches in the center of the garden or from an overlook platform complete with rocking chair.

This children's garden—the only one of its kind in the United States—was conceived and designed by Jim Folsom, Marge and Sherm Telleen Director of the Huntington Botanical Gardens, and Ned Kahn, an award-winning kinetic artist from Sebastopol, California.

Raven sculpture, above, overlooks magnetic sand exhibit in foreground; conservatory rises in background. Rollicking topiary bears, right, are among several animal-shaped trees and shrubs in the garden.

· THE ROSE HILLS FOUNDATION ·
CONSERVATORY FOR BOTANICAL SCIENCE
AN INTERACTIVE SCIENCE CENTER

LEFT: A view of the Rotunda where tropical plants are featured

ABOVE: *Amorphophallus titanum* in flower

IN THE CONSERVATORY more than fifty interactive exhibits offer a rare opportunity to study a wide range of plants from all over the world. The exhibits are divided among four galleries. Three of the galleries focus on specific habitats: tropical rain forest, misty mountain forest, and mossy wetland. A fourth gallery, called the Plant Lab, provides an introduction to botany, with exhibits on roots, stems, leaves, flowers, spores, and seeds to touch, smell, measure, and observe using a variety of scientific instruments, including compound and dissecting microscopes.

The tropical rain forest in the Rotunda hosts one of the world's most unusual plants: *Amorphophallus titanum*, commonly referred to as the "world's largest flower," or "the stinky plant." Native to the equatorial forest of Sumatra, where it is known as the "corpse flower" because of its smell, the plant made botanical history in 1999 when it bloomed at the Huntington, the first-ever flowering of the rare plant in California and only the eleventh-recorded bloom in the United States. Other tropical plants exhibited in the Rotunda include unusual palms, fruit trees, begonias, giant water lilies, climbing vines, and orchids.

The Cloud Forest Gallery is cool and misty. Here the presentations show plants that live with their roots in the air instead of the soil as well as the unusual pollination methods of orchids. In the mossy wetlands of the Bog Gallery are carnivorous plants of the temperate coasts, including Venus flytraps, sundews, pitcher plants, and butterworts. The exhibits demonstrate how these plants lure and digest insects.

Extraordinary plants that can't be grown outside in Southern California fill the Conservatory's galleries. From top, counterclockwise: flowers of *Medinilla* species; cones of the cycad *Zamia neurophyllidia*; flower of a *Tillandsia* bromeliad species; flower of the spiral ginger *Costas ocae*.

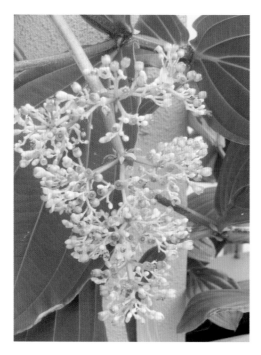

The Conservatory building was inspired by a Victorian-style lath house built on the property in the early twentieth century. The structure, which served as part nursery, part storage, and as a display space for palms, ferns, rhododendrons, and cyclamens, had an openwork construction of redwood slats that allowed filtered sunlight and ample circulation of outside air. In contrast, the new Conservatory has a steel frame covered by glass panels that provide 50 percent shade for the plants inside. The wings have a maximum interior height of 26 feet, and the Rotunda is 96 feet across with a 43-foot tall dome. A sophisticated computerized system controls the climate.

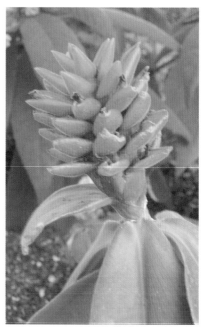

OPPOSITE: Endless discovery awaits visitors amid the amazing diversity of cloud forest plants.

Hang the leaves
in your own
patterns

The Conservatory is a place for the exploration of plants: from examining beautiful shapes and textures to observing strange and marvelous adaptations.

OPPOSITE: The leaf quilt in the Plant Lab.

FROM TOP LEFT, CLOCKWISE: Discovering Spanish moss *Tillandsia usneoides*; tropical pitcher plant *Nepenthes* species; the modified leaves of a *Sarracenia* pitcher plant; a tiny *Maxillaria* orchid; the carnivorous *Sarracenia purpurea*.

· LIU FANG YUAN, THE GARDEN ·
OF FLOWING FRAGRANCE
A POETIC RETREAT INSPIRED BY CHINESE TRADITION

Craggy rocks found in the garden come from Lake Tai, near Suzhou, China.

A CONTEMPLATIVE JOURNEY through Liu Fang Yuan 流芳園 begins with a stroll along the undulating Wall of the Colorful Clouds 景雲壁, which slopes down toward the garden's south entrance. Lattice windows offer glimpses into an enchanting world of tiled-roof pavilions and corridors, arched and zigzag bridges, and craggy rocks. Luscious floral scents waft from within, calling to mind the garden's name: Liu Fang Yuan, or Garden of Flowing Fragrance. *Fang*, meaning "fragrance" in Chinese, refers to the aromas of flowers and trees. *Liu*, or flowing, describes the movement of pleasant scents in the garden, or *yuan*.

Inside the wall, the shimmering Lake of Reflected Fragrance 映芳湖 provides the garden's focal point. Set in a natural depression for water runoff, the lake reflects the trees and structures and attracts visiting herons, egrets, and ducks. Weathered limestone rocks from China's Lake Tai 太湖 frame the water's edge.

Liu Fang Yuan opened to visitors in early 2008 to highlight Chinese plants and traditional Chinese architecture and culture. It emulates the refined style of private gardens constructed in Suzhou, China, during the Ming (1368–1644) and Qing (1644–1901) dynasties.

Designed by Jin Chen, a Chinese-American landscape architect, the garden reflects the philosophy of the

Fish finial from the Bridge of the Joy of Fish.

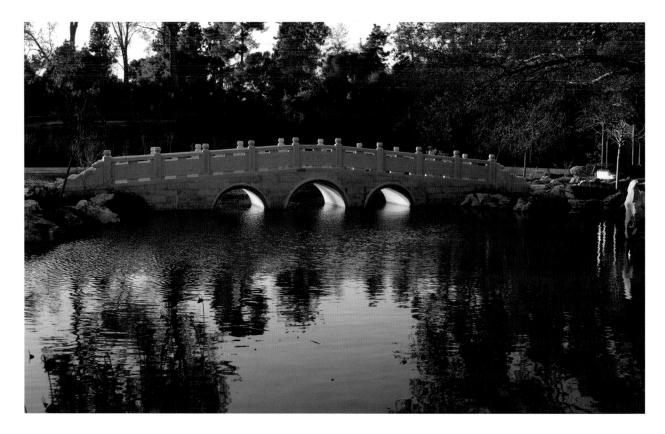

The Jade Ribbon Bridge extends gracefully over the Lake of Reflected Fragrance.

seventeenth-century Chinese painter and garden designer Ji Cheng, who wrote that garden builders should preserve elements of the chosen site while creating new landscape compositions and views. The garden's aesthetic depends upon exact spatial proportions and refined, handcrafted details. Much of the construction was done by master craftsmen from Suzhou, where nearly all the building components were created, including roof tiles, wood, paving stones, granite bridges, and decorative carvings.

In keeping with Chinese garden tradition, Liu Fang Yuan's buildings, courtyards, and bridges have individual names with rich cultural associations. The Terrace of the Jade Mirror 玉鏡臺, for instance—its round gates shaped like the full moon—is inspired by Chinese literature, in which the moon is compared to a round mirror of highly prized white jade. The Hall of the Jade Camellia 玉茗堂, a tea house, refers to a plant closely associated with China: *Camellia sinensis*, the tea camellia. This small-leaved, small-flowered camellia is grown for its leaves, which are harvested to make tea. In several of the garden's structures, camellia motifs and wood carvings emphasize the importance of tea to Chinese cultural traditions.

Scrolls of poetry, written in beautiful calligraphy, offer further layers of meaning. A couplet hanging in the Love for the Lotus Pavilion 愛蓮榭 reads, "Though rooted in the mud, how could the lotus be sullied? / Its fragrance spreads far with even greater purity." The Pavilion for Washing Away Thoughts 滌慮亭—a thatched-roof hut next to a stream leading to the Japanese garden—suggests nature's gift of

Liu Fang Yuan is situated in an ancient grove of oaks and pines native to California.

serenity to the visitor: "Flowing water can purify the mind. / Fragrant mountains are good for quiet contemplation."

Botanical motifs decorate many of the structures, including the hexagonal, double-storied Pavilion of the Three Friends 三友閣. The "three friends of the cold season" are plants that thrive in cold weather: pine, bamboo, and a plum known as *mei hua* (*Prunus mume*). The pavilion's circular ceiling is carved with motifs of these three plants, which represent courage and tenacity. The bamboo and pine are resilient evergreens, and the plum offers its beautiful white and pink blossoms in January, regardless of the weather.

Liu Fang Yuan, surprisingly, is the only truly seasonal garden at the Huntington. Its blossoms begin soon after Chinese New Year, when the forsythia brings abundant showers of golden flowers. From March through May, a play of peach, plum, cherry, forsythia, and peony unfolds amid the green of pendulous willow branches and the burgundy of emerging maple leaves.

Summer, filled with the scents of gardenia and michelia, also brings the dramatic white blossoms of the lotus. The lotus's plate-like leaves create a canopy above the water surface, punctuated by the plant's large, star-like flowers, which mature into flat-topped pods.

Autumn ushers in another round of spectacular color: the gold of ginkgo, the fire of pistache, and the bronze of sweetgum. These trees are especially striking during the season: the maidenhair tree, *Ginkgo biloba*, easily recognized by its

The Wall of the Colorful Clouds, or Jing Yun Bi, calls to mind *jingyun,* brightly colored clouds that are harbingers of good fortune.

fan-shaped leaves, and the Chinese pistache, *Pistacia chinensis,* which produces a small, round red nut. The garden's *Liquidambar formosana,* native to Asia, and its near relative, *L. styraciflua,* native to North America, both bear lobed leaves, similar in appearance to those of the maple. Unlike the maple, these sweetgums produce seed in woody, spiked fruiting balls that cover the ground in early winter.

A grove of ancient trees includes numerous specimens of California's native coast live oak, *Quercus agrifolia,* purposefully incorporated into the garden's design in acknowledgment of their age and beauty. The coast live oak can be distinguished by its medium to small dark green and shiny leaves, whose cupped edges have occasional holly-like spines. Near the Terrace of the Jade Mirror is a young example of *Q. acutissima,* an oak species from China.

To the west and north is a towering pine forest rich with *Pinus torreyana* from Southern California, *P. halepensis* from Europe, and *P. canariensis,* native to the Canary Islands. The smaller, trained pines in the garden are the Asian *P. thunbergii.*

Liu Fang Yuan would not be complete without the mulberry, a tree that has influenced Chinese culture and industry as the food source for silkworms. A handsome mulberry provides shade on the slope above the Listening to the Pines bridge, each spring producing a crop of soft, fuzzy, heart-shaped leaves.

OPPOSITE: Entrance to the Plantain Court, or Ba Jiao Yuan.

163

The ceiling of the Pavilion of the Three Friends contains motifs of the "three friends of the cold season"—pine, bamboo, and plum—plants that have long been identified in Chinese literature and art as symbols of unity, courage, and tenacity.

The Love for the Lotus Pavilion is an elegant open building that looks out over the Pond of Reflected Greenery.

· THE ENTRANCE ·
AND PARKING GARDENS
A VISITORS PAVILION AND PARKING AMID PLANTING

Tabebuia chrysotricha extends its yellow trumpet flowers in the March sunshine above an underplanting of lavender.

This escutcheon atop a pair of wrought iron gates at the seldom-used Euston Road entrance bears the arms of the Carew family. The gates came from Beddington Park, Surrey, England, where they were erected by Sir Nicholas Carew in 1714.

ARRIVING VISITORS first park in a lot softened by islands of greenery in the blacktop and plantings of background trees and shrubs. At twenty-five acres, a sixth of the Huntington's public area, this garden holds twelve hundred cars with little of the wasteland effect of most parking lots. South of the lot a small, more formal green garden is planted with podocarpus, coast redwood, sycamore, magnolia and a line of carrotwood trees (*Cupaniopsis anacardioides*). It serves as prelude, inviting visitors into an entrance pavilion. That in turn acts as a kind of vestibule to a broad terrace and a small plaza beyond, planted to bright seasonal flowers, flowering trees, and lofty palms, overlooking the grand sweep of gardens to the south.

In the northeast part of the estate, the parking lot was at first a kitchen garden, a place for growing fruits and vegetables and raising poultry, and also a test plot for Chinese date, grapefruit, pistachio nut, persimmon, and other exotic fruits. In 1908 Henry Huntington began planting in the northern half of this area what is believed to be California's first commercial avocado grove. Some gnarled veterans with massive trunks remain, still producing fruit. The arboretum aspect of avocado cultivation continues as new trees are planted in a growing collection of historical cultivars north of the parking lot in a

RIGHT: A pink silk floss tree (*Chorisia speciosa*) shades changing seasonal displays of annuals.

FAR RIGHT: *Pittosporum rhombifolium* has small white flowers in spring followed by long-lasting clusters of showy orange berries in the fall and winter.

cooperative effort with the California Avocado Society, which deposited its records at the Huntington in 1992.

Later the ground south of the avocado grove became a test planting of rare eucalyptus and other Australian trees, which remained in place long enough to achieve mature size. In 1966 the area was opened to the public as a general arboretum, and in 1979 it became a parking lot related to the pavilion, which opened two years later.

Thirty-two islands and peripheral dividers that define the lot's parking bays and lanes are planted to mostly drought-tolerant trees, shrubs, and ground covers. They preserve specimens from the former avocado orchard, fruit tree planting, and arboretum, and also display new material from a continuing planting program. The central section of the lot contains the Australians, the large eucalyptus and such others as bottlebrush (*Callistemon*), grevillea, and senna (*Cassia*). Another veteran from the old test planting is cork oak (*Quercus suber*) from the Mediterranean.

A central walkway in the southern third turns spectacular in late spring with the blue-violet bloom of jacaranda trees (*Jacaranda mimosifolia*) that line it on both sides. The garden has two Huntington tree introductions, strawberry snowball (*Dombeya cacuminum*) and flowering cherry (*Prunus serrulata* 'Pink Cloud'). Other flowering trees and their colors are silk tree (*Albizia julibrissin*), pink; orchid tree (*Bauhinia purpurea*), varicolored pink; fringe tree (*Chionanthus retusus*) and snowdrop tree (*Halesia diptera*), both white; princess tree (*Paulownia tomentosa*), blue; tulip tree (*Liriodendron tulipifera*), pale green; and golden trumpet tree (*Tabebuia chrysotricha*), yellow.

LEFT: White silk floss tree (*Chorisia insignis*) blooms in the heat of summer, from August to October.

Among other tree plantings are tipu tree (*Tipuana tipu*) from South America, maidenhair tree (*Ginkgo biloba*), and several cultivars of sweet gum (*Liquidambar styraciflua*).

· LANDMARK TREES ·
LARGE, RARE, COLORFUL, OLD

Trees are a vital part of this landscape, interesting as individuals and awe-inspiring as a collection. A thousand native oak trees and specimens of more than forty introduced oak species, many notable for their rarity or unusual size, grace the gardens. The deciduous English oak, *Quercus robur*, at left is uncommon in California.

RIGHT: The Alexandra palm (*Archontophoenix alexandrae*), which has a dramatically striped trunk, will reach ninety-five feet in the rain forest. A native of Australia, it was named for Princess Alexandra of Denmark.

OVER THE DECADES, many of the Huntington's trees have become landmarks for their unusual size, age, rarity locally or nationally, or for having notable flowering or other features. Some had a head start toward landmark status, for Henry Huntington encouraged William Hertrich to bring in specimens as mature as he could find—or move. Hertrich devotes a section of his *Personal Recollections* to adventures in moving and planting large trees without the use of modern equipment. Indeed, his pioneering experience with such transplanting was put to practical use in large-scale landscaping for the 1915 expositions in San Diego and San Francisco. Today the Huntington has an assemblage of landmark trees, some of them the only examples or the largest of their kind, some the parents of trees in other gardens.

South of the entry pavilion, several specimens of silk floss tree (*Chorisia speciosa*), Queensland kauri (*Agathis robusta*), and Senegal date palm (*Phoenix reclinata*) serve as introduction to garden delights to come. In the lawn beyond, three of the most impressive oak specimens on the grounds are English oak (*Quercus robur*).

Some of the Huntington Gallery's landmark trees include a large specimen *Talauma hodgsonii*, a magnolia relative from the Himalayas, and a tall, white-flowered *Chorisia insignis*, from the

The beautiful lemon-scented gum (*Eucalyptus citriodora*) was a favorite of Henry Huntington's, who asked that this species be planted by his mausoleum. The smooth white bark emphasizes the tree's elegant structure from afar, and close up, it has a pleasing, powdery-white surface—until it sheds its bark every summer. Crush the leaves and the lemon fragrance is unmistakable.

RIGHT: The evergreen cork oak (*Quercus suber*) will grow as high as it is wide. Its bark is exceptionally thick and able to regenerate after cork has been cut from a new layer that forms each year. In commercial groves, the bark is harvested for cork after twelve years' growth.

upper Amazon basin in Peru, adjoining the loggia, and a massive, century-old English yew (*Taxus baccata* 'Elegantissima') south of it. Another large flowering tree is seen east of the building: Moreton Bay chestnut (*Castanospermum australe*) from Australia.

The rose garden has three monumental Montezuma cypress (*Taxodium mucronatum*), trees grown from seed Hertrich collected from Chapultepec Park in Mexico City in 1912. A giant of this species, "El Tule," in the state of Oaxaca, is Mexico's largest and probably oldest tree. Two other conifers stand out for great size in the rose garden. A Queensland kauri (*Agathis robusta*), planted in the 1890s by the San Marino Ranch's previous owner then transplanted in 1908 despite its forty-foot height to make way for the mansion, stands out for great size in the rose garden. Also near the restaurant is *Magnolia delavayi,* one of the few evergreen magnolias from Asia hardy in Southern California.

In the subtropical garden grows a large Italian stone pine (*Pinus pinea*) well sited to reveal the full drama of its form. Among the subtropical garden's large collection of flowering trees an old and distinguished cape chestnut (*Calodendrum capense*) stands out when covered with blossoms in the summer.

Several brachychitons are in the Australian garden: *Brachychiton rupestris*, identified by its swollen trunk, and *B. discolor*, planted in a grove, striking for great quantities of rosy-pink bell-shaped blossoms in summer. The Australian garden also has many significant eucalyptus, some unusual for great size, especially *Eucalyptus tereticornis.*

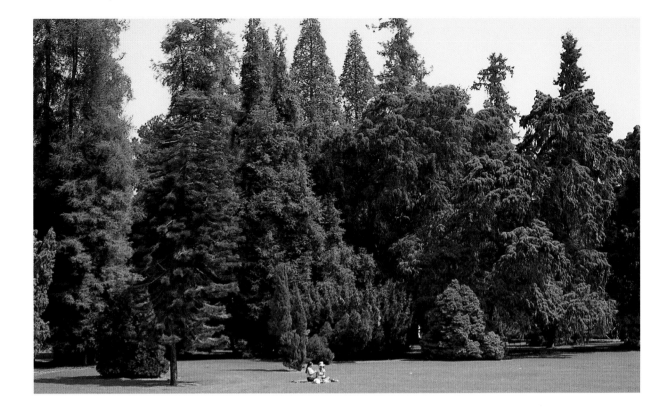

The conifer collection west of the lily ponds has several landmark trees. One is known to be the largest specimen in the United States, Taiwan redwood (*Taiwania cryptomerioides*), a cypress relative native to Taiwan and China, planted in 1908. Growing here are the largest examples on the grounds of deodar cedar (*Cedrus deodara*) from the Himalayas, and southern magnolia (*Magnolia grandiflora*)—though the tallest specimen of the latter grows at the southwest corner of the Huntington Gallery. Also of note are araucarias, tall Southern Hemisphere cone-bearing trees native to South America, Pacific islands, and Australia; two tall species here are *Araucaria cunninghamii* from Australia and *A. angustifolia* from Argentinia and Brazil.

A landmark at the edge of the jungle garden is one of the oddest trees in any of the gardens, an ombú (*Phytolacca dioica*) from Argentina, a gnarled old veteran with a giant swollen base. Also in the jungle garden, three *Ficus macrophylla* var. *columnaris* are notable for their height.

In the palm garden, the rare Chilean wine palm (*Jubaea chilensis*) is still one of the most impressive. Also known for their rarity are the windmill palms (*Trachycarpus martianus*), native to the Himalayas and the most mature specimens in a public garden in Southern California.

Not a tree, perhaps, but the desert garden's patriarch cactus, a *Cereus xanthocarpus*, mature when originally planted, weighs in at an estimated fifteen tons. Taller and more treelike, an outstanding specimen dragon tree (*Dracaena draco*) has grown to such heroic size its heavy limbs need steel-pipe props.

Lacy foliage and nut-like cones of *Calocedrus formosana*

In the northern area, a blue Atlas cedar (*Cedrus atlantica* 'Glauca') at the junction of Botanical Circle and Palm Drive is one of the largest in Southern California and the parent, through cuttings, of most blue Atlas cedars distributed by nurseries in the region. And Palm Drive is lined with a particularly fine planting of Guadalupe Island palm (*Brahea edulis*).

Among parking lot trees, one landmark is *Calocedrus formosana*, a rare conifer from Taiwan, in the southwest section. Many of the larger specimen trees are eucalyptus species from a 1920s test plot and avocados from an earlier planting.

Opposite: This specimen of *Taiwania cryptomerioides* is the largest in the United States.

RIGHT: In the background is one of the largest specimens in the United States of *Dracaena draco*, the dragon tree of the Canary Islands. This is one of the oldest plants in the desert garden, acquired in 1912 and part of the original garden. The low mass in the foreground is *Puya coerulea* var. *violacea*. To the left is a monstrose cereus, *C. horribarbis*. The aloe on the left is *Aloe camperi* 'Cornuta', one of the hardiest, showiest, and most disease-resistant aloes in the garden.

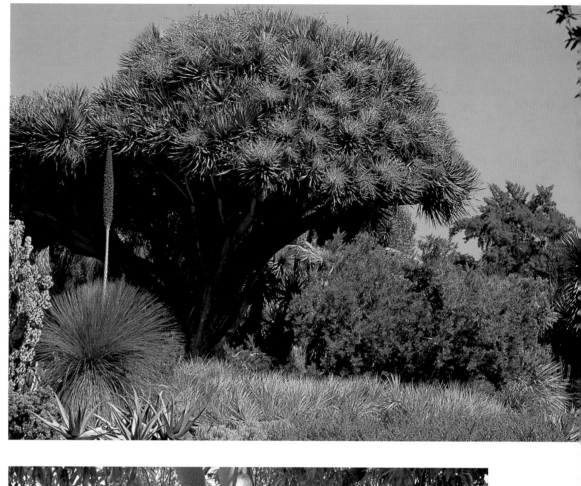

Brachychiton rupestris of Australia is called bottletree after its swollen trunk.

LEFT: The ombu tree (*Phytolacca dioica*), planted in 1914, has a thick crown of leathery leaves. Its enlarged base is a water-storage device that evolved for survival on the plains of its native Argentina. It can reach sixty feet in height and nearly that in width.

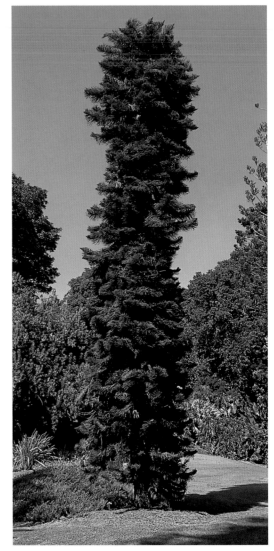

Above: This hybrid of *Araucaria columnaris* is aptly named for its columnar form.

Left: This splendid Queensland kauri (*Agathis robusta*) was planted in the 1890s, then moved as a mature forty-foot tree to make room for the new Huntington mansion.

Opposite: Montezuma cypress (*Taxodium mucronatum*) is evergreen in mild climates, although the old foliage falls in early spring as the new leaves appear. Its weeping branches and slender leaves make a graceful tree that may attain great stature with age.

TOP: *Cassia spectabilis* carries a generous crop of bright yellow flowers at the end of summer, in August and September.

BELOW AND RIGHT: The emergence of the first delicate and scented blooms of deciduous magnolias is a welcome winter sight. The Huntington collection comprises mostly small trees, with flowers ranging in color from white through pink to purple-pink.

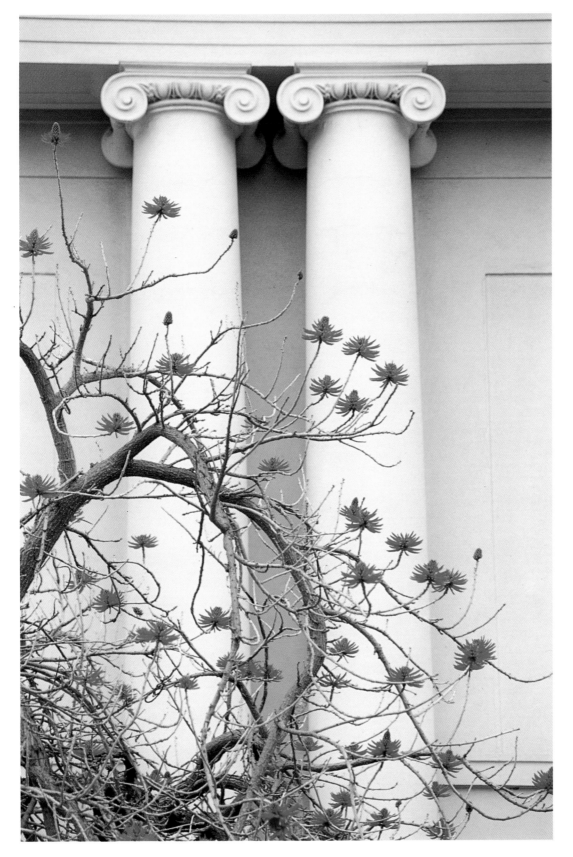

The Library's smooth Ionic columns are the backdrop for this coral tree (*Erythrina coralloides*). From spring until winter its red flowers are visited regularly by hummingbirds.

· ADORNMENTS TO THE GARDENS ·
TEMPLES, SCULPTURE, FOUNTAINS, ACCESSORIES

Floribunda roses 'French Lace' surround the Temple of Love in the rose garden. A structure from a dependency of the Palace of Versailles, it was possibly designed by Jacques Ange Gabriel (1710–1782) for the Versailles gardens. Inside is the eighteenth-century stone sculpture *Love the Captive of Youth,* by or after Louis-Simon Boizot (1743–1809).

IN THE GRAND European tradition, fountains, sculpture, and accessories embellish the Huntington gardens. More than three hundred such objects in stone, metal, and wood, many of them eighteenth century, some more recent, serve as focal points, accents, or merely adornments. Four are in the tempietto, or "small temple" genre, of which the largest and most imposing is the Huntington mausoleum, reminiscent in form and scale of Donato Bramante's celebrated 1502 Tempietto in Rome—so influential a Renaissance structure that it undoubtedly was part of architect John Pope's education. Three smaller, light-hearted temples contain sculptures on the theme of love: at the south end of the North Vista, in the rose garden, and on the south lawn below the Huntington Gallery. A bronze Saint Francis stands beside the lily ponds. The finest sculptures are placed near the Library and the Huntington Gallery, while the most impressive display is an array of stone figures lining the North Vista. Large ornaments include two elaborate fountains, in front of the Library and at the focal point of the North Vista. Smaller fountains are seen at the entrance and on the Huntington Gallery's north and west sides.

Among seventy other garden accessories, in the Japanese garden are such special touches as an arch bridge and a classical zigzag bridge, a bell pavilion, and stone lanterns, statues, pagodas, and votary tablets. More than a hundred benches are disposed throughout the gardens in carefully chosen, agreeable spots, some of carved marble but mostly of wood, many of them memorials to individuals. The inventory of garden adornments also includes carved or molded stone and ceramic urns and planters, freestanding pillars, ornamental gates, and pavilions for shade and rest.

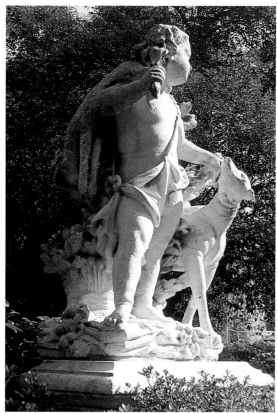

TOP LEFT: The stunning red-flowering spear lily (*Doryanthes palmeri*) blooms at the foot of Persephone, daughter of Zeus and Demeter, installed near the north door of the Huntington Gallery. The 1750 stone statue is from the Hofburg (the imperial palace) in Vienna.

TOP RIGHT: Depicted with flowing hair and a thick mustache, this limestone Mars, part of the North Vista statuary, is framed by *Camellia japonica* 'Glen 40 Variegated'.

BOTTOM LEFT: Half dog, half lion, Koma-inu is one of a pair of stone guardian figures outside the Japanese garden. Here as in Japan, their mission is to stand guard at important places.

BOTTOM RIGHT: With his game slung over his shoulder, a young boy and his dog return from the hunt. The eighteenth-century stone statue marks the entrance to one part of the camellia collection.

OPPOSITE: The Huntington mausoleum traces its roots back to classical Greece with its Ionic columns, to classical Rome with its shallow-profile dome like that of the Pantheon, and to Renaissance Italy with its form reminiscent of Bramante's sixteenth-century Tempietto in Rome.

Benches in the rose garden include an ornately carved double settee in marble, top, and two wooden ones in front of the bougainvillea-covered wall of the Huntington Gallery, right. Sphinx detail from a marble bench by mausoleum, above.

Wooden benches are strategically placed for special views throughout the gardens, like the one, above, overlooking a collection of golden barrel cacti in the desert garden and the one at right in the Shakespeare garden. A concrete seat, left, was built into the hillside in a shady glade in the Japanese garden.

Ferocactus latispinus

Det. by: Héctor M. Hernández   Date: April 1992
Collector, No. & Date:

Ferocactus

MEXICO: Puebla. Rte 135, 5.6 km S of
Coxcatlan, along roadside. Alt. 1050

· RESEARCH AND EDUCATION ·
THE GARDENS' IMPORTANT MISSION

One of the nine thousand specimens in the herbarium, this *Ferocactus latispinus,* a kind of barrel cactus, was collected along a road in the Mexican state of Puebla in 1985.

M ORE THAN A BEAUTIFUL garden-park with interesting planting, the Huntington Botanical Gardens aims to advance the understanding and appreciation of plants and gardens, a mission defined in 1926 by founder Henry E. Huntington.

Specific goals are to maintain the historical character of the gardens, especially those of traditional design around the Library and Huntington Gallery, to interpret estate landscaping and aesthetics as Huntington envisioned them, to preserve some of the original estate grounds, and to present a continuing horticultural display of plants for Southern California gardens. Programs, exhibits, literature, and new collections, sometimes developed with participation from the library and art departments,

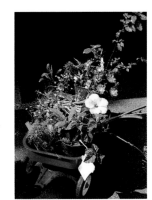

Red wagons are the conveyances of choice during the popular annual plant sale in May. The Huntington propagates plants for sale all year long. Garden enthusiasts come from long distances to buy plants not always found in nurseries.

reinforce the institution's interest in history, literature, and art, while similar efforts address public education in plant biology, the importance of biodiversity, and appreciation and conservation of plants.

The botanical division acquires and curates plant collections, emphasizing those related to existing theme gardens. They test and distribute new plant material, with a special interest in little-known and endangered species, in developing ideas about plant cultivation and landscaping, and in conserving plant biodiversity. They collaborate with scientists and professionals in plant study and make resources and plant material available to researchers and institutions. Staff members do research, concentrating on areas related to the Huntington's gardens, and publish the results.

Research was an early priority and William Hertrich tested many kinds of plants for suitability to Southern California, including the first successful outdoor planting of orchids. His records of plant survival and losses during major freezes and other data are still useful today.

In 1963 Hertrich's successor Myron Kimnach established a herbarium specializing in plant groups and geographic regions related to the gardens. It provides a permanent record of the gardens' plants, documents collecting expeditions, and holds specimens for taxonomic study. Succulent plants make up its most numerous category; others are plants from the New World tropics, from the world's arid regions, and plants of horticultural importance from wild collections.

Today the gardens attract researchers in botany, taxonomy, and plant physiology, molecular and cellular biology, and hybridization. University and independent scientists have used the plant and herbarium collections for such varied projects as monographs on the genera *Chamaedorea* and *Conophytum*; anatomical research on columnar Mexican cacti, on the wood of Didiereaceae, and on *Welwitschia*; analysis of the latex of euphorbias for industrial applications; and extraction and cloning of *Welwitschia* RNA for enzymes important to cone development.

The garden periodically publishes an *Index Seminum*, a list of seeds native to Southern California and from the gardens' exotic plants, for exchange with other institutions around the world. They in turn receive more than 240 such lists, some of them seed sources for the Huntington.

Educational activities fall into two main categories, interpretation of the gardens and public programs. Onsite garden programs reach schoolchildren, home gardeners, horticulturists, botanists, and others. For example, a Reading Plants class introduces fourth through seventh graders to differences among plants of the jungle, desert, and aquatic gardens. Another explores the cultural significance of various aspects of the Japanese garden. University instructors may use the gardens as an outdoor classroom or laboratory. And the gardens provide intern work-study experiences for college students and young professionals in horticulture and botany.

LEFT: Arms loaded with plant materials, including huge bamboo sheaths, students head for the school bus after a garden class.

RIGHT: Students pick plant specimens like this succulent on docent-led class in the gardens called "Reading Plants," a comparative study of desert, jungle, and aquatic environments.

Other programs include annual symposia on the study and cultivation of succulents and roses. Lectures and plant sales introduce enthusiasts and home gardeners to landscaping, plant culture and selection, and historical and modern plant varieties. Horticultural societies and garden clubs present public shows of azaleas, camellias, succulents, bonsai, and flower arranging. And a corps of trained docents lead regularly scheduled garden tours, or booklets are available for visitors who prefer to structure their own exploration of this botanical wonderland.

· THE BOTANICAL LIBRARY ·
BOOKS RARE AND OLD, NEW AND FAMILIAR

This etching of *Rosa gallica* is one of ninety hand-colored plates in the first book devoted just to roses, *A Collection of Roses from Nature* by Mary Lawrence (1797).

RIGHT: Hand-painted bird of paradise *(Strelitzia reginae)* by Syd Edwards appeared in *The New Flora Britannica,* published in London in 1806.

T HE HUNTINGTON'S botanical library consists of a working reference library in the Botanical Center and a collection of rare and important volumes on horticulture and botany kept in the stacks of the Library. In building one of the world's finest libraries in the fields of English and American history, literature, and science, Henry Huntington collected rarities in botanical books mainly when he bought whole collections and private libraries that included them. Since his death, acquisitions of other rare and valuable books have created a sizable special collection in the early history of science, some of it occasionally displayed in the Library's exhibition hall.

The earliest materials are from the fifteenth-century printing revolution that followed the appearance of Gutenberg's Bible, the first book printed with movable type. How botany as a science eventually developed from general knowledge and speculation can be traced in early treatises from first editions of Linnaeus, Darwin, and others. The collection is especially strong in herbals of the sixteenth and seventeenth century, among them works by Otto Brunfels and Leonhart Fuchs, pioneers in drawing from live plants to illustrate their books. Such early works

White magnolia is one of 100 color plates from drawings by George D. Ehret in *Plantae Selectae* issued in Germany 1750–73 and published by the botanist, bibliographer, and eminent physician Christoph Trew.

RIGHT: A color illustration of a sunflower from *Phytanthoza Iconographia* (1737–45) by Johann Weinmann

on plants and gardens as the first book on the oak tree, by Duchoul, and Jean Robin's florilegium, or compendium of known American and New World plants, also link the Huntington's interest in literature, art, and botanical material. So do eighteenth- and early nineteenth-century botanical garden catalogs that document the emergence of exotic and New World plants and manuals from the same period that instruct the artist in flower drawing and painting. Succulent plants are treated in rare editions of classical works by Engelmann, Haworth, and Lemaire, names perpetuated in plant names. Two seminal editions on roses are the eighteenth-century *A Collection of Roses from Nature*, by Mary Lawrence, the first book devoted exclusively to the rose, and the 1820 *Les Roses*, by Pierre Joseph Redouté, famous for its illustrations.

The library has a complete collection of *Curtis's Botanical Magazine*, starting from the late eighteenth century. The first, greatest, and longest continuously published botanical magazine, it chronicles a dazzling array of discoveries from the pre-Victorian era to our time. In the same company are the sumptuously illustrated, nineteenth-century *Edwards' Botanical Register* and Sir Joseph Paxton's *Magazine of Botany*, along with the later *Gardener's Chronicles*.

The botanical reference library, in daily use by the staff, contains important general books and journals but emphasizes materials useful for the identification,

This cereus cactus with its flower and fruit—another plate from *Plantae Selectae*—is also the work of Ehret, a noted eighteenth-century botanical illustrator. The plates were engraved and hand colored by J. J. and J. E. Haid.

study, and cultivation of plants in the Huntington's major gardens and collections. Areas of concentration include camellias, roses, and succulents; Australia, southern Africa, and Japan; tropics, especially of the New World; and dry-lands floristic and ecological studies. The library also contains gardening, landscaping, culture, botanical, horticultural, and taxonomic general reference materials.

The library of the Cactus and Succulent Society of America is housed here. Newsletters from plant societies across America and "round robin" letters, which contain detailed information on plants for specific climates, propagation, growing tips, and the like, are on file, as are correspondence and ephemera from botanists and seed and nursery catalogs from the nineteenth century on.

CALENDAR OF COLOR
A Changing Pageant of Flower and Foliage Displays Every Season of the Year

WINTER

The Tournament of Roses, perhaps the world's greatest annual floral spectacle, launches the New Year in nearby Pasadena. In the Huntington's rose garden, pruning is put off until after that so holiday visitors can enjoy the season's last flowers. In January camellias come into their own as reticulatas and then japonicas follow sasanquas already in bloom. Wisterias soon burst forth on arbors in the Japanese garden, while fruit trees flower pink and white there and in the Shakespeare garden. The showiest color of all explodes in the desert garden as aloes produce their red, orange, and yellow flower clusters. Acacias and other Australian trees and shrubs come into flower, while South African bulbs begin year-long color on the ground. Deciduous magnolias begin blooming, as do showy Hong Kong orchid, Taiwan cherry, pink snowball, coral, and other trees.

SPRING

A transition from winter's bright and sunny or sometimes rainy days to the frequently overcast days of late spring, April brings out peak bloom in several gardens. Roses are in full flower, the Shakespeare garden—a color showcase like the entry pavilion's south garden—sports its finest blooms, the North Vista is enlivened with camellias and azaleas, the herb garden has hollyhock and other flowers, and in the Australian garden the curious little kangaroo paw makes its spring appearance. Such flowering trees as bottlebrush, cassias, cape chestnut, and grevillea stand out as individuals while an avenue of jacaranda in the parking lot garden creates a blue-purple color mass. In the desert garden, yuccas and similar plants put forth big flower stalks, cacti show flashy blooms, and beds of flowering ground-cover succulents dazzle with some of nature's most intense hues.

Trumpet tree (*Tabebuia chrysotricha*)

Chinese fringe tree (*Chionanthus retusus*)

Kaffir lily (*Clivia miniata*)

Camellia hybrid, 'Beverly Baylies'

Prunus 'Pink Cloud'

Floribunda rose, 'Orangeade'

Opuntia littoralis

Jacaranda

Azalea

SUMMER

Beds of lavender agapanthus spread color across the ground along with cannas, daylilies, salvias, and other flowers in the subtropical garden. The evergreen Delavay and grandiflora magnolias bloom white, casting heavy scent on the summer air. In front of the Library bright red flowers of Bidwill's coral tree attract hummingbirds by the drove. In other gardens color comes from lacebark bottle tree, cassias, Moreton Bay chestnut, crape myrtle, oleanders, and—toward the end of summer—pink and white silk floss trees. If it seems hot in the desert garden, where yuccas and puyas still bloom in July, seek out the cooler lily ponds, where lotus and water lilies are in full flower, and the jungle garden next to that area, where bright red gingers bloom in the shade of tall trees.

AUTUMN

Heralds of fall, the sasanquas are the first camellias to bloom, from October on. Look for foliage color in the parking lot garden and other spots, but mostly in the Japanese garden, where maples take on varied hues and the grove of ginkgo turns a bright yellow. Other yellows come from flowering cassia trees in the Australian, subtropical, and parking lot gardens. The last roses of summer hang on in their own garden while in December the first aloes and crassulas begin their winter color in the desert garden and the purple Mexican sage puts on its own show in the subtropical garden. Lending yuletide notes, hollies are laden with bright red berries in the Shakespeare and other gardens, and red poinsettias flaunt their colorful bracts near the south terrace of the Huntington Gallery.

Bird of paradise (*Strelitzia reginae*)

Gladiolus dalenii

Sweet olive (*Osmanthus fragrans*)

Daylily (*Hemerocallis*)

Firewheel tree (*Stenocarpus sinuatus*)

Mexican sage (*Salvia leucantha*)

Cereus huntingtonianus

Airplane plant (*Crassula falcata*)

Index

Page numbers in bold refer to illustrations

THE BOTANICAL GARDENS AT THE HUNTINGTON
was produced by Perpetua Press, Santa Barbara
Designer: Dana Levy
Editor: Letitia Burns O'Connor
Typeset in Berkeley Oldstyle and Michelangelo
Printed in China
by Toppan Printing Company